what the actual f! from pubes to boobs & everything in between

Funny, No-Panic Survival Guide to Parenting
Tweens Through Puberty - Hormones, Mood
Swings, Body Changes, and Real-Life Conversations

Growing Up Chronicles

contents

this is for you

To my two world-changers, Mara and Bash — my brilliant, bewildering, endlessly surprising daughter and son who've taught me more about resilience, humor, and the power of a sweet treat bribe than any parenting manual ever could. Watching you navigate voice cracks, impromptu dance challenges, and dramatic closet cleanout (because nothing fits anymore) has been the most incredible adventure (and the best comedy show) of my life. You remind me every day that growing up is messy, magical, and absolutely worth celebrating.

And to every parent out there riding the tween tidal wave — this book is for you. For the late-night DMs, the sympathetic head nods when picking up from a playdate, or the "I-feel-you" text threads when the day was a struggle — may you find here the encouragement to keep going, hacks to keep you (mostly) sane, and enough laughs to power you through the next unexpected eye-roll or digital drama. We're in this together — celebrating the small triumphs, getting through the big meltdowns, and cheering one another on every step of the way.

To Simeon — my partner in everything, including the chaos. Thank you for being the calm to my storm, and the person who reminds me daily that we're doing okay, even when it doesn't feel like it. I couldn't survive tweendom — or anything else — without you.

And to Ally — who suggested this book be called "From Pit to Tits". I cleaned it up slightly, but the spirit remains. Thank you for the laughs, the honesty, and for proving that the best parenting advice often comes from friends who are just as confused as you are.

With all my heart — and a lifetime supply of humor to get us parents through this crazy journey!

one
welcome to the tweenosphere

Buckle up, parents: you're entering a land where logic takes a vacation, hormones play bumper cars, and everyday objects suddenly become "embarrassing." Welcome to tweendom! Just yesterday, my daughter Mara declared that wearing matching socks was "cringe," and my son Bash asked if deodorant was "technically a vegetable since it grows under your arms." This is our new reality – and somehow, we're supposed to navigate it with grace, wisdom, and enough coffee to power a small village.

Meet "The Actual 'F'"

So, what does the "F" really mean? Throughout this book, it represents the full spectrum of tween parenting reality. Sometimes it's Fear – like reading their search history and finding "How to survive a parent meltdown," suddenly wondering who's teaching whom. Other times it's Flush – when you (or your tween) feel your cheeks go beet-red during an innocent talk about periods over breakfast cereal.

The F could be Families – because we all get to ride this rollercoaster together, even if we sometimes prefer a nice, predictable merry-go-round. It might be Frustration when they insist vegetables are "basically poison" or Funny when they ask if

gravity is "technically optional." Sometimes it's Forge ahead –
your daily mantra for survival – or Forgive, both yourself and
them, for that time you both hid in the bathroom crying.

Perhaps most often, it's the raw F-word – the unfiltered scramble
of emotions, surprises, and "what-are-we-even-doing?" reactions
that hit when your child steps into this bewildering stage. In
truth, it's all of the above, often simultaneously, usually when
you're running late for school.

This book isn't a perfect parenting manual because those don't
exist. It's a survival guide written by someone currently in the
trenches, offering permission to laugh at the beautiful chaos,
practical hacks tested on real tweens, and validation that you're
not alone in this wild ride. This book won't judge your family's
unique brand of chaos or suggest one-size-fits-all solutions,
because every tween is wonderfully, mysteriously weird in their
own way.

Believe it or not, humans have been freaking out over puberty
since medieval times, when parents gave their kids cabbage leaf
compresses to soothe mysterious itchiness. Your own parents
probably dealt with VHS tapes of "The Facts of Life" and giant
'telephone' books for researching "the birds and the bees." Today,
we have TikTok "puberty hacks" and AI chatbots answering
questions we're too embarrassed to ask our pediatricians.

Regardless of era, each generation has grappled with the same
fundamental question: How do I guide my child when their body
and brain feel like they're staging a revolution from the inside
out? The answer, it turns out, is the same across centuries: with
patience, humor, and the acceptance that none of us really knows
what we're doing.

Humor helps us survive in ways that parenting manuals never
mention. Laughter isn't just the icing on the tween-parent
survival cake – it's your parachute when you feel like you're free-
falling into uncertainty. Whether you're giggling at the absurdity
of your tween's dramatic reaction to broken Wi-Fi or sharing

belly laughs over their latest philosophical observations about why cereal is "basically soup," humor keeps you grounded. Lean hard into silliness, because when your tween tells you they're "literally dying inside" because their phone battery hit 20%, the last thing anyone needs is a neuroscience lecture about emotional regulation.

Giving Yourself Grace (You're Not Failing)

Here's the secret every parent needs embroidered on their favorite coffee mug: everyone feels awkward during their child's tweendom – kids and parents alike. Picture yourself transforming from the calm, collected adult you were five minutes ago into someone frantically Googling "Is it normal for my kid to apply lip gloss to their eyelids?" This disorientation isn't a personal failing – it's the natural response to watching your child become someone you're still getting to know.

You have permission to be imperfect. You'll forget permission slips, serve cereal for dinner more often than you'd like to admit, and use "because I said so" despite swearing you never would. You'll also create magical moments, provide precisely the right hug at exactly the right time, and somehow manage to raise a human being who will eventually thank you for surviving their tweendom (though probably not until they're thirty).

Give yourself permission to laugh at the chaos, perhaps with a strategically hidden chocolate stash, and remind yourself that this phase is temporary. Besides, someday you'll tell grandchildren about "that time I accidentally called my kid by the dog's name during a meltdown," and it will be a family legend rather than personal embarrassment.

Remember that you're not just managing a tween – you're learning to parent one. There's no instruction manual for the specific combination of personality, hormones, and cultural timing that is your unique child. Be patient with yourself as you figure out what works, because your learning curve is just as steep as theirs, and significantly less acknowledged by society.

The Great Awkwardness

If you've ever caught your tween standing at the mirror, whispering, "Why does my nose look weird today?" they're not auditioning for a detective movie. They're experiencing the Great Awkwardness that comes with becoming a tween: part child, part mini-adult, and entirely bewildered by their own existence.

One day, they're eating mac and cheese with the unselfconscious joy of a six-year-old; the next, they're trying to apply concealer to their first pimple with the serious concentration of a surgeon. They're tall enough to reach the top kitchen shelves but still trip over their own feet with impressive regularity. Emotionally, they'll cycle through "Mom, you're the worst!" and "Mom, I need to talk" within the same breath, leaving you wondering if you need whiplash insurance.

Your internal monologue during this phase might sound like: "Is this normal? Did I traumatize them yesterday by suggesting they shower? Am I still cool? How quickly can I Google 'signs of normal tween behavior' before they notice me panicking?" Here's a gentle reality check: if maintaining your "cool parent" status is your primary goal, you've already lost that battle. Instead, embrace your inner detective – complete with mental notepad for tracking strange new behaviors – but remember to collect data with empathy rather than the investigative subtlety of a police interrogation.

During peak awkwardness moments, keep emergency supplies handy. Tissues for mysterious tears that appear without warning, snacks for sudden hangry meltdowns, humor for defusing tension, patience for yourself when you don't understand their latest issue, and sweet treats because someone in this equation needs to maintain their sanity.

Puberty 101: A Quick Primer

Before venturing deeper into this adventure, let's cover the biological basics. Think of this as your CliffsNotes version of what's about to happen, minus the awkward textbook diagrams that somehow make everything more confusing.

Puberty isn't the simple "growth spurt" many of us imagine. If only it were as straightforward as shooting up six inches overnight and calling it done. Instead, it's a series of physical, emotional, and social changes that your tween will unlock like achievements in a video game they never signed up to play. Hormones flood their system like surprise guests at a dinner party, kicking off changes in voice, hair growth, mood regulation, and more. This process typically lasts anywhere from two to five years, depending on genetics, nutrition, and whether your tween is mysteriously powered by a diet consisting primarily of Kraft Mac & Cheese and optimism.

The hormone situation resembles an army mobilization, with estrogen and testosterone as the commanding officers. When these chemical messengers surge through your child's system, they don't arrive peacefully. Expect voice cracks worthy of a horror movie sound effect, tears set off by cereal commercials about family togetherness, and the emergence of a mysterious aroma that can only be described as "Eau de Tween Body Odor." While you can't negotiate with hormones or convince them to follow a more convenient schedule, you *can* arm yourself with facts. Deeper voice? Completely normal and temporary. Sudden passionate interest in graphic novels about mushroom kingdoms? Also normal – if baffling.

Tweens hit milestones on their own timelines, and that timing can shape their experience in a big way. Kids who start changes around ten or eleven may feel like early pioneers in uncharted territory, while those who begin around twelve or thirteen might worry they're falling behind their peers. Both experiences are normal, and both come with real emotional challenges – just ones that call for tailored support and reassurance (and the occasional reminder that puberty is not, in fact, a competitive sport with trophies).

When gathering information about these changes, resist the urge to fall down Google rabbit holes that lead to forums with titles like "My kid thinks vegetables are toxic – is this puberty?" Instead, bookmark reliable sources like your pediatrician's website, established health organizations, and evidence-based parenting resources. Knowledge truly is power, but misinformation wearing a medical-sounding costume can create more anxiety than clarity.

Your Tween: The New Frontier

Now that you understand the biological landscape, let's address the bigger question: who is this person standing in your living room, wearing mismatched socks and sporting an expression that suggests they're contemplating the meaninglessness of existence at 3:45 on a Tuesday.

Your tween inhabits a world with rules you've never heard of, where Snapchat streaks carry more weight than laundry schedules, where one poorly chosen GIF could theoretically end their social life, and where consuming the last slice of pizza without permission represents a fundamental breakdown of civilized society. They're constructing their identity faster than you can research "best tween haircuts," which means their moral compass spins like a disco ball, pointing toward brilliance one minute and complete chaos the next.

Understanding their digital native reality helps explain some of their seemingly irrational behavior. Your tween doesn't remember a world without smartphones, social media, or instant access to information and entertainment. What feels overwhelmingly fast-paced to you may be their normal speed of life, so your suggestions to "slow down" or "be patient" might sound like asking them to function in slow motion.

When logic appears to take extended vacations from your household, expect delightfully unexpected scenarios. You'll plan a family dinner for six o'clock, and they'll insist they physically cannot eat until seven-thirty, then demolish a Toaster Strudel™

at six-oh-five. You'll suggest they walk the dog, and they'll suddenly volunteer for extensive household chores — but only the ones they can livestream on TikTok. One moment, they're reciting Shakespeare with surprising eloquence, and the next, they're convinced that Mr. Darcy would never hold doors open because "that's not authentic to his character development." Accepting this beautiful randomness becomes essential for your mutual survival.

Building empathy for their experience requires recognizing that understanding doesn't mean agreement. When your tween sobs over Wi-Fi connectivity issues or declares that wearing deodorant feels like "being attacked by chemical weapons," you don't need to share their perspective completely. You just need to validate their experience while gently holding boundaries and reality checks.

Try responding with phrases like "I can see this is really important to you" instead of launching into detailed explanations about your own childhood hardships. Remember that empathy isn't about having all the answers or fixing every problem — it's about acknowledging their feelings while helping them build coping strategies for a world that can feel bigger and more complicated by the day.

Fasten Your Seatbelts

You've now earned your "Welcome to the Tweenosphere" badge by understanding the many meanings of "F," recognizing that hormones operate like rogue armies, and accepting that logic will regularly take unscheduled vacations from your household. You've also learned that empathy doesn't require complete comprehension and that humor often provides better solutions than lectures.

Most importantly, you've been reminded that you're not alone in this adventure. Every parent throughout history has watched their child transform from the familiar little person they knew into someone mysterious, wonderful, and occasionally baffling.

Your job isn't to prevent this transformation or control every aspect of it – it's to provide steady support, unconditional love, and enough laughter to get you both through the turbulence.

In the next chapter, we'll explore the specifically boy-focused aspects of this journey – voice changes that sound like dying walruses, mysterious hair growth in unexpected places, and the delicate art of introducing deodorant as a daily life necessity, because if I have to remind Bash one more time, I'm going to start billing him for my therapy sessions. Before we venture there, take a moment to appreciate how far you've come just by picking up this book and committing to understanding your tween's experience. That commitment alone puts you in the "Parent of the Year" category, even when it feels like you're barely surviving each day.

Remember...if parents managed to guide children through tweendom with dial-up internet and VHS-based health education, you can absolutely handle this challenge with WiFi, Google, and a sense of humor about the beautiful absurdity of raising humans.

two

pubes to pectorals: the boy edition

One minute, your son is speaking like a regular human. Next, his voice cracks into a sound that could summon dogs three blocks away. Add hair growth with chia-pet-level commitment (who remembers those?), and a body that now seems to run on glitchy settings controlled by someone wearing oven mitts. Welcome to the boy side of puberty, where logic goes out the window, physics becomes optional, and your sweet child transforms into someone who can grow three inches overnight but still can't figure out how to walk through doorways without colliding with the frame. It's like watching a nature documentary about someone you used to know, except the narrator has clearly lost their mind and the wildlife has moved into your house.

The Voice of Doom: When Vocal Cords Stage a Revolution

Your son's voice used to be that adorable, slightly nasally sound that could call "Mom!" from across crowded playgrounds? Well, prepare for that voice to be replaced by what sounds like a bullfrog with seasonal allergies attempting to perform Broadway show tunes.

The 'Great Vocal Transformation' rolls in like a slow-moving freight train, and your living room is about to become ground zero for acoustic events that would make seismic equipment jealous. Scientists have yet to fully explain how the human larynx can produce sounds that simultaneously resemble bullfrog mating calls and construction equipment experiencing mechanical failures.

Voice changes follow a predictable pattern of unpredictability. During the pre-crisis phase, he still sounds mostly like himself with occasional wobbles that hint the vocal apocalypse is approaching. You might notice his voice getting slightly deeper when he's tired, like a recording played at the wrong speed, or catching subtle cracks when he gets excited about something – usually food or a playdate with his bestie.

The initial crackle phase brings genuine acoustic surprises that catch everyone off guard, including him. He'll yawn and produce a sound somewhere between a foghorn and a dying moose, then immediately return to his normal voice as if nothing happened. These early voice breaks often occur at inappropriate times, such as in silent classrooms or quiet restaurants, creating maximum embarrassment.

The chaotic seesaw stage tests everyone's patience and sense of humor. Sentences bounce between two wildly mismatched vocal registers: "Mom, can you buy me – " followed by something that sounds like Darth Vader clearing his throat, then back to normal for " – a new video game?" During this phase, asking him to repeat himself becomes a daily ritual, so settle in.

Eventually, his voice settles into its new, deeper register during the emerging bass phase. This transition often catches parents completely off guard when answering phone calls, suddenly hearing an unfamiliar voice saying "Hello?" and wondering if you dialed the wrong number.

Supporting him through voice changes requires the patience of a saint mixed with the perfect poker face. When he unleashes a particularly spectacular throat-clearing roar mid-conversation, resist the urge to giggle, applaud, or offer commentary that might be preserved in family legend forever. Instead, continue the conversation as if everything is normal.

Hair Today, Gone Tomorrow: The Great Sprouting Adventure

Puberty approaches hair growth like an enthusiastic gardener who's lost all sense of planning, proportion, and aesthetic judgment. One day, your son's face is baby-smooth; the next, bristles erupt with the determination of weeds breaking through concrete, appearing in places you never expected and growing at speeds that defy botanical science.

The pubic hair development saga begins with what can only be described as "sparse landscaping by someone who's never seen a lawn." Early growth typically starts with wispy hairs that resemble dandelion fuzz more than anything requiring actual attention. He might not even notice these initial changes, which works in your favor since it gives you time to prepare for conversations that will make everyone involved wish they had chosen another topic.

As development continues, these hairs thicken and darken with the enthusiasm of plants receiving miracle fertilizer, forming increasingly noticeable patterns that can send self-consciousness skyrocketing – right up there with catastrophic social embarrassments. This stage often coincides with a growing awareness that his body is becoming something new compared to what he's always known.

Armpit hair development poses the most immediate practical challenges because it directly affects the family's indoor air quality. In simpler times, parents could hope their children would shower occasionally and leave armpit management to natural selection. Modern tweens require more strategic intervention because their armpit situation can potentially evacuate entire rooms faster than fire alarms.

Facial hair development adds another layer to the experience, transforming your child into someone who looks like they're wearing a disguise made of scattered pepper flakes. That first "teen beard" might look sophisticated in his imagination, but reality often resembles what happens when someone applies fake facial hair using a glue stick and questionable judgment.

The patchy growth pattern creates some truly avant-garde facial-hair moments. He might develop a mustache that looks like it was sketched by a distracted toddler, or chin hair that seems to be following instructions from an entirely different manual. The asymmetrical nature of early facial hair creates fascinating topographical maps that change daily.

First shaving experiences require more preparation than space missions and often produce results that suggest razors might be alien technology designed to confuse earthlings. Teaching proper shaving technique to someone whose coordination is still adapting to recent growth spurts creates learning opportunities that test everyone's patience and first aid knowledge.

The Aroma Chronicles: Eau de Tween Jungle

Say goodbye to the days when his only distinctive scent came from leftover pizza residue, dirt from outdoor adventures, or that mysterious smell that children develop after playing outside for extended periods. Welcome to the era of Tween Jungle, a fragrance so distinctive it could probably be trademarked and sold as a biological warfare deterrent.

Body odor development follows its own timeline, often appearing before he's mentally prepared to meet adult grooming requirements. Genetics plays a significant role – if you or your partner developed noticeable body odor around age twelve, prepare for similar aromatic adventures with your son, possibly with interest compounded.

The deodorant conversation usually begins with you noticing that your once-sweet child now emanates an aroma that could clear rooms faster than fire alarms while simultaneously attracting every neighborhood dog within a three-mile radius, yet remains completely oblivious to this olfactory development. It's like living with someone who's developed a superpower they don't know they possess and wouldn't want if they did. But when you gently suggest they might benefit from some underarm assistance, they respond with genuine confusion, as if you've suggested they start speaking ancient Latin or performing interpretive dance.

They'll argue that deodorant is "unnatural" and "full of chemicals," conveniently forgetting that they regularly consume beverages with ingredient lists that read like advanced chemistry textbooks and snacks with ingredient lists longer than their homework assignments.

The application process turns into a daily comedy routine worthy of a late-night monologue. They'll use approximately half a stick in one enthusiastic swipe, creating what appears to be sidewalk chalk art under their arms, or they'll apply such a microscopic amount that it serves no practical purpose beyond making them feel they've fulfilled their parental compliance obligations.

Teaching proper deodorant technique requires more patience than coaching a room full of kindergartners and more show-and-tell energy than a YouTube tutorial host. You'll find yourself creating step-by-step tutorials, drawing diagrams that explain coverage patterns, and developing analogies that compare deodorant application to other familiar activities unrelated to personal hygiene.

They'll forget to apply deodorant roughly 85% of the time, creating situations where you become the family's unofficial smell-detection specialist, casually suggesting "touch-ups" before social events while trying to maintain everyone's dignity. You'll develop supernatural abilities to detect missed deodorant applications, typically during car rides when escape is physically impossible.

The scent selection process reveals personality traits you never knew existed and preferences that defy logical explanation. They might choose something called "Arctic Blast" that smells like a combination of mint toothpaste and regret, or "Ocean Breeze" that bears no resemblance to any ocean you've ever encountered and wouldn't fool anyone who's actually experienced marine environments.

Growing Pains: When Bodies Become Foreign Objects

The relationship between tweens and their rapidly changing bodies is like someone attempting to operate complicated machinery using an instruction manual written in a language they're still learning. Simple tasks that were once automatic now require conscious thought and strategic planning worthy of an elite coach drawing up a game plan.

You'll witness collisions with stationary objects that seem to move when he's not looking, creating bruises and minor injuries that suggest your furniture has developed aggressive tendencies.

The rapid changes in physical proportions turn everyday movement into accidental Cirque du Soleil auditions. Jeans that fit perfectly last week suddenly resemble capri pants. At the same time, his favorite t-shirts transform into unintentional crop tops that reveal more midriff than anyone in your family signed up for. His relationship with clothing becomes a daily reminder that nothing in life is permanent, especially fabric.

Doorways become natural enemies that seem to narrow specifically when he approaches them. The physics of teenage navigation defy logical explanation. Somehow, someone can grow six inches taller but still misjudge the amount of space required to pass through openings they've successfully navigated thousands of times before.

The relationship between the brain and body during this period resembles a communication system experiencing technical difficulties. Messages that should travel instantly from intention to execution now seem to get lost in translation, creating delays that affect everything from catching thrown objects to completing high-fives.

The teenage growth spurt creates a fascinating paradox: someone can grow half a foot in six months yet still be unable to find objects directly in front of them. Their visual perception appears to lag behind their physical development, leading to search-and-rescue missions for items in plain sight.

His appetite expands proportionally to his growth rate, transforming him into what appears to be a human garbage disposal with sophisticated taste preferences. He can eat enough food to sustain a small village and still claim he is starving five minutes later, creating grocery bills that belong on a national budget spreadsheet.

The Awkward Awakening: What Nobody Warns You About

Now we're venturing into territory that makes many parents want to hide under blankets and pretend this conversation isn't necessary. Still, unfortunately, surprise erections are an inevitable part of male puberty, arriving without warning and causing mortification that's hard to top in adolescence.

Morning erections represent the most predictable version of this phenomenon, though calling them predictable is like calling earthquakes scheduled events. Inappropriate dreams or thoughts don't cause these – they're simply blood flow doing its biological job with all the subtlety of a marching band practicing in a library.

When he stumbles out of his bedroom looking confused and embarrassed about mysterious overnight developments, resist the urge to provide detailed biological explanations or make jokes that will haunt family gatherings for decades. Instead, respond with the same matter-of-fact tone you'd use to discuss the day's schedule or what's on the grocery list.

The timing of unexpected erections seems designed by someone with a cruel sense of humor and detailed knowledge of when embarrassment would cause maximum psychological damage. They'll appear during math class, family dinner, church services, or any other situation where discretion is essential, and bathroom breaks require elaborate explanations.

Public erection panic can turn an ordinary moment into a full-blown emergency drill. He sits down, stands up, and suddenly finds himself in a situation that requires immediate strategic thinking and creative problem-solving, which his developing brain isn't yet ready to handle.

Teaching discreet management strategies is a life-skills lesson no parenting manual adequately prepares you for. You'll find yourself explaining techniques like strategic backpack placement, the art of sitting down quickly, and the art of excusing himself gracefully, which is honestly a life skill that will serve him well beyond puberty.

The bathroom break strategy becomes an essential survival skill that requires more planning than a 10-course meal. He needs to learn how to excuse himself politely without elaborate explanations while maintaining the appearance of casual normalcy, which is quite an achievement when you think about it.

Discussing this topic requires balancing educational information with age-appropriate reassurance, keeping the kind of straight face you've been perfecting since he was a toddler asking why the dog doesn't wear pants. You're basically providing sex education without the dramatic presentations, using the same tone you'd employ to explain how to change a tire or balance a checkbook.

Final Thoughts: Surviving the Boy Transformation

You've now navigated the essential territory of boy puberty – voice changes that sound like construction equipment, hair growth in previously unexplored territories, coordination challenges that turn simple tasks into extreme sports, surprise anatomical developments, and odor management that requires the strategic planning of a cross-country road trip with no bathroom stops.

Remember that these changes represent significant milestones in his journey toward becoming a young man – even when it feels like you're watching him morph into a brand-new life form right before your eyes. Your calm, supportive presence during this time teaches him that these developments are routine, manageable, and nothing to be ashamed of, despite their tendency to create household comedy.

Every challenge he faces now – physical awkwardness that makes simple tasks feel impossible, social navigation that requires new skills, emotional growth that nobody prepared him for – builds the foundation for his adult relationship with his own body and identity. Your role involves providing steady guidance, unconditional love, and enough humor to help both of you survive the transition without losing your minds.

This phase is temporary, even though it may last until he's eligible for retirement benefits. Your patience and understanding now create the groundwork for lifelong communication and trust, plus you're collecting material for embarrassing stories that will entertain family gatherings for decades to come.

three
from boobs to blooms: the girl edition

W elcome to the stage where bra shopping requires the logistical coordination of a cross-country move, mood swings can hit with roller-coaster whiplash and flip without warning, and friendship drama unfolds with so many twists it could power a full season of reality TV. This is the girl edition of tween puberty, where every day brings new adventures in emotional plot twists, where your daughter transforms from the child you knew into someone magnificent, mysterious, and occasionally capable of achieving dramatic performances that would make Broadway actors jealous. It's like living with a brilliant artist who's constantly rewriting the script while you're still trying to figure out what play you're supposed to be in.

The Breast Quest: From Plains to Peaks

Ah, breasts: those mysterious developments that suddenly dominate cafeteria conversations and turn casual clothing shopping into a full-on engineering project – complete with measurements, support systems, and bargaining that feels like haggling at a chaotic street market.

One day, your daughter barely notices her chest; the next, she's monitoring her development with the intensity of a scientist tracking important climate data, creating detailed mental maps of changes that occur faster than continental drift but feel more dramatic than geological epochs.

Breast development follows what doctors call predictable stages, though explaining them to your daughter requires more skill than scientific terminology. The journey begins during the "flat earth" phase when everything sits flush against her chest, and she might occasionally wonder when she'll start looking like the older girls at school who seem to have unlocked mysterious biological achievements.

The bud sprouting phase brings the first fundamental changes, often appearing as small, sometimes tender bumps that feel like her body is conducting secret experiments without consulting her first. These breast buds represent significant milestones that deserve acknowledgment without dramatic fanfare. However, explaining this to someone experiencing their first body rebellion requires the calm confidence of a surgeon and the gentle honesty of a best friend.

As development continues, breast tissue grows outward from her chest wall with the enthusiasm of plants receiving miracle fertilizer, creating increasingly noticeable changes that affect clothing fit, self-consciousness, and the family's bra-buying budget. This phase often initiates requests for bras, marking a transition that feels both exciting and overwhelming for daughters and parents who suddenly realize they're navigating uncharted territory together.

The almost-there phase adds extra layers as various features develop their own distinct quirks, creating that strange in-between where she's nearing her "grown-up" version while still trying to process the emotional and practical reality of living in a body that seems to change faster than she can keep up with.

Bra shopping deserves recognition as one of the most potentially fraught adventures in parent-child relationships, rivaling driving lessons and college selection processes for sheer potential to create lasting family trauma. This expedition involves navigating sizing mysteries that seem designed by people who enjoy mathematical confusion, style decisions that reflect her developing identity, and comfort requirements that change daily based on activities, confidence levels, and whether Mercury is in retrograde.

Sizing involves deciphering numbers, letters, and measurements that change faster than her shoe size and make about as much sense as cryptocurrency exchange rates. Most stores now offer tween-specific options labeled with simple size categories, but prepare for the inevitable moment when she declares that every available option either looks like medieval armor or feels like torture devices designed by people who've never encountered actual human anatomy.

Training bras serve as a gentle introduction to this new clothing category – usually soft cotton styles without underwires or any of the heavy-duty structural features of more supportive bras. Making the shopping experience enjoyable by letting her choose patterns and colors that reflect her personality becomes essential – whether she gravitates toward bows, geometric designs, or a color palette that could spark a spirited debate on a home makeover show.

The underwire decision arrives when she reaches more advanced development stages and begins requesting "real bras" like older friends who seem to have mastered adult female mysteries. This transition requires introducing the concept of support versus comfort and helping her understand that adult women have debated this topic for centuries without reaching unanimous conclusions.

Period Panic: The Monthly Subscription Nobody Signed Up For

When menstruation arrives, it does so with a flair for dramatic timing that seems specifically designed by someone with intimate knowledge of when embarrassment would cause maximum psychological impact. Midnight discoveries, frantic supply searches, and urgent whispered conversations become part of your new reality as she navigates this significant milestone.

Predicting first periods involves watching for several indicators that suggest Mother Nature is preparing to send formal invitations to monthly biological events that will continue for the next several decades. Breast tenderness may present as reports of her chest feeling "weird" or uncomfortable, particularly during certain mysterious times that seem to follow their own unpredictable schedule.

Cramping and bloating in her lower abdomen, especially when accompanied by general digestive weirdness, often precede menstrual cycles by several months, creating symptoms that can be confused with various other conditions until patterns become clear. Mood fluctuations that seem more intense than typical tween emotional variations can signal hormonal changes preparing for menstruation. However, distinguishing these from typical tween drama is basically advanced pattern recognition with no answer key.

White vaginal discharge, which might initially concern her, actually represents normal development that typically appears months before her first period, providing a warning that biological changes are progressing according to schedule, even when that schedule seems designed by someone with a questionable sense of timing.

Preparing for this milestone involves both practical supply gathering and emotional readiness conversations that require more finesse than a surgeon. Rather than waiting for the event to begin, initiate these discussions when you notice early signs of development, allowing her time to process information and ask questions without the pressure of immediate need.

Product education is essential before she faces quick decisions in potentially stressful moments when clear thinking may be compromised by panic or embarrassment. Pads offer the easiest introduction to menstrual management since they require no insertion techniques and provide visible confirmation of proper placement. However, explaining this to someone who has never considered such logistics requires patience and creativity.

Tampons are a more advanced option that many girls prefer for sports and swimming, but introducing them is most effective with calm, clear guidance that pairs practical how-to support with age-appropriate information. Start with slender or junior sizes. The instruction diagrams inside the box are genuinely helpful – review them together if she's comfortable, or let her figure it out privately with the door closed and your reassurance that questions are welcome.

Menstrual cups appeal to environmentally conscious families and offer long-term cost benefits, but they typically work better for girls who are already comfortable with tampon insertion and have established regular cycles. Saving cup conversations for later in her menstrual journey, when she's gained confidence with simpler options, prevents overwhelming her with too many choices during initial learning phases.

Emergency preparedness involves more than just having supplies available – think less 'grab a pad' and more 'deploy supply caches across multiple locations. Assembling period starter packs for her backpack, your car, and key locations throughout your home creates backup systems that prevent minor inconveniences from becoming major catastrophes.

Managing period accidents requires planning and calm responses when inevitable mishaps occur, because physics and timing conspire to create situations where she needs supplies exactly when they're least convenient or accessible. Teaching her to carry spare underwear, showing her emergency coverage techniques, and establishing protocols for seeking help build confidence that reduces panic during stressful moments.

HAIR WARS: The Great Follicle Rebellion

Your daughter's relationship with body hair will likely feel more layered than you remember, shaped by personal preference, peer influence, cultural expectations, and practical choices that shift as her identity and social awareness grow.

Pubic hair development follows predictable biological patterns, but it can spark unpredictable emotions and big questions about what to do next – even for the most unflappable adults. When friends start debating grooming choices with the seriousness of a five-year life plan, she might feel pressured to decide before she's ready or comfortable with the available options.

The pubic hair conversation requires gentle guidance that explains all available options – trimming, shaving, or embracing natural growth – while emphasizing that these choices remain entirely personal and completely revisable as her preferences and comfort levels change over time.

When she expresses interest in shaving, providing education on proper techniques rather than simply forbidding the practice prevents unsafe experimentation and builds trust. Showing her how to use small trimmers with adjustable guards for length control, explaining the importance of clean, sharp razors, and demonstrating that gentle application of shaving cream protects sensitive skin while building confidence.

Leg hair decisions often arise when she notices differences between her appearance and that of older girls or women in the media, creating self-consciousness about natural development that previous generations might not have experienced at this age. If she wants to start shaving her legs, consider a gradual approach, starting with one leg to practice, and keep backup plans in place in case of mishaps.

Armpit hair conversations require balancing normalcy with practical considerations of peer social dynamics and personal comfort. While body hair serves natural functions, including trapping deodorant and helping regulate scent, she may feel social pressure to conform to grooming expectations within her friend group.

Facial hair concerns typically involve light peach fuzz that might become more noticeable as she develops, creating anxiety about appearance changes that feel beyond her control. Reassuring her that some facial hair is completely normal while teaching gentle cleansing techniques helps build confidence without suggesting that natural appearance requires dramatic interventions.

The key to all body hair conversations involves emphasizing her autonomy over her own body while providing education about safe practices and realistic expectations. Helping her understand that grooming choices reflect personal preference rather than moral requirements builds confidence in decision-making while ensuring she knows that these choices can change as she grows and her priorities evolve.

Mood Meteorology: From Sunny Skies to Category 5 Emotional Hurricanes

Emotional intensity during a girl's puberty often resembles weather systems that meteorologists would classify as requiring emergency preparedness protocols and possibly evacuation procedures. One minute, she's peacefully reading in her room; the next, she's sobbing because you suggested that brussels sprouts exist in the world and might occasionally appear on dinner plates.

Hormonal fluctuations create genuine physical and emotional changes that deserve recognition rather than dismissal, even when those changes seem to defy all logical explanation and turn your living room into a one-person theatrical production. Estrogen surges can crank sensitivity way up, so casual comments like "your hair looks different today" can set off reactions you'd expect after genuinely bad news.

Random emotional reactions range from uncontrollable giggles over things that aren't particularly funny to dramatic proclamations about the meaninglessness of existence triggered by minor inconveniences like slow Wi-Fi connections or slightly wrinkled clothing. These reactions reflect real neurological changes rather than attention-seeking behavior, though explaining this to someone in the middle of an emotional tornado requires timing and patience.

Understanding these mood changes helps you address underlying stress rather than just addressing surface complaints that may not reflect the actual source of distress. When she declares, "You don't love me," and immediately transitions to "I hate everyone," she's processing intense feelings with limited experience of emotional regulation rather than making considered assessments of family relationships or global humanitarian issues.

Managing mood emergencies requires recognizing intensity levels and responding with strategies appropriate to each phase of emotional buildup. Minor fluctuations may need nothing more than patience and space for her to process feelings independently, while moderate emotional storms often benefit from gentle validation and comfort, such as favorite snacks or a cozy environment.

Major meltdowns require crisis management know-how that prioritizes safety and connection over immediate problem-solving or logical reasoning. During peak emotional intensity, focusing on staying calm yourself, ensuring she doesn't harm herself or others, and providing a steady presence without attempting to fix everything immediately often works better than detailed explanations or rational discussions.

Self-esteem and body image challenges intensify during this period as she compares herself to filtered social media images, peers who develop at varying speeds, and impossible beauty standards that affect even adult women who should know better. Social media platforms bombard her with perfectly curated content that makes real life feel inadequate by comparison, creating unrealistic expectations about daily appearance and lifestyle presentation.

Reality-check strategies include educating her on photo editing, filters, and the significant gap between online presentation and daily life. Showing her unfiltered celebrity photos, discussing the time and effort required to create "perfect" social media content, and helping her curate feeds that emphasize body positivity and diverse representation provides a perspective that counters impossible standards.

Building authentic self-worth requires focusing on her abilities, character, and achievements rather than commenting exclusively on appearance or comparing herself to others. Acknowledging her kindness toward friends, celebrating her creative projects, recognizing her academic efforts, and emphasizing the multiple ways she contributes positively to her family and community build confidence based on genuine accomplishments rather than external validation.

Friendship Politics: Social Navigation in the Digital Age

Tween girl friendships can be so tangled that they make a group text with 45 relatives planning Thanksgiving dinner look calm, logical, and well-organized. Social dynamics shift faster than stock market fluctuations; today's best friend can become tomorrow's source of complicated drama, and group chat politics require negotiation tactics that most adults haven't developed despite decades of experience.

The BFF phenomenon creates intense loyalty bonds that feel more significant than family relationships when things go well and more devastating than romantic breakups when relationships shift. Your daughter may experience friendships that consume most of her emotional energy, making conflicts particularly painful and reconciliations extraordinarily meaningful, which in turn affects her overall mood and daily functioning.

Social media raises the stakes because interactions can happen nonstop, not just during school hours. Group chats, story posts, and digital communication create twenty-four-hour social environments where drama can develop and escalate without natural cooling-off periods. What begins as an innocent miscommunication can escalate into reputation-damaging gossip that undermines multiple friendships simultaneously, spreading faster than anyone can contain it.

Exclusion dynamics cause some of the deepest pain during this developmental stage because social belonging can feel essential to survival, not just a nice bonus. Being left out of group activities, excluded from social media interactions, or dropped from friend groups can bring on real grief responses that deserve serious acknowledgment – not minimizing comments about how friendships are "temporary" (even if your adult brain is quietly thinking, *"You've known her for nine minutes."*).

Mean girl behavior often disguises itself as humor or casual comments that carry significant social impact, even when they appear relatively innocent to outside observers. Backhanded compliments, deliberate exclusion, rumor-mongering, and digital harassment can cause lasting damage while offering plausible deniability, making intervention challenging. Teaching her to recognize these patterns helps prevent her from accepting mistreatment as normal in friendships.

Help her distinguish between typical friendship friction and genuinely problematic behavior. Friends sometimes accidentally hurt each other's feelings, make choices that feel like rejection, or go through periods when they're less available due to their own circumstances. These situations differ from patterns of manipulation, consistent criticism, or deliberate cruelty.

Teaching her to recognize manipulation involves role-playing scenarios, discussing healthy relationship patterns, and empowering her to set boundaries with friends who consistently make her feel bad about herself. Help her understand that real friendships involve mutual respect, support, and kindness rather than constant competition or criticism – a foundation that will serve her in adult relationships too.

Building empathy skills helps her navigate complex social situations while maintaining her own emotional well-being. Encouraging perspective-taking through discussing characters' motivations in books and movies, participating in community service, and practicing small acts of kindness builds emotional intelligence while providing positive outlets for social energy.

When friendship drama inevitably lands in your living room as an emotional crisis, see Chapter 4's section on Friendship Fiascos for guidance on how to support her through the immediate fallout.

Celebrating the Beautiful Complexity

You've now navigated the essential territory of girl puberty – breast development adventures that require an engineering degree, menstrual prep that feels like stocking an emergency kit, body-hair decision-making on par with a company handbook debate, emotional intensity that could stump a seasoned air-traffic controller, and social dynamics that make spy thrillers look straightforward.

Remember that these changes represent your daughter's journey toward becoming a remarkable young woman – even when it feels like she's reinventing herself in real time while directing her own one-person Broadway show. Every challenge she faces now – physical adjustments that require daily adaptation, social navigation, and emotional growth that no one fully prepares for – builds resilience, empathy, and strength that will serve her throughout life.

Your steady presence, unconditional love, and willingness to navigate these uncharted waters together provide exactly what she needs during this transformative time, even when you feel like you're making up the rules as you go. The girl standing in your living room, alternating between needing your guidance and asserting her independence with dramatic flair, is becoming someone wonderful who will eventually thank you for surviving her tweendom with humor and grace.

Trust the process, maintain your sense of humor, and remember that this intensity is temporary, even though it sometimes feels like it might outlast your mortgage. You're not just surviving daily drama – you're helping someone develop the emotional intelligence and essential lessons they'll need as adults, one mood swing and friendship situation at a time.

four
an emotional rollercoaster ride

Consider this your warning label: this chapter includes seatbelts, airbags, a lifetime supply of tissues, and a direct line to emergency chocolate. Hormone-driven mood swings can hit like natural disasters, and your tween may become the epicenter of beautiful, chaotic emotions that make an instruction manual feel like a fairy tale. Understanding tween emotions requires instincts that would make storm chasers envious, while simultaneously earning advanced degrees in crisis negotiation and possibly theoretical physics, since the laws of emotional cause-and-effect seem to operate according to principles that science hasn't discovered yet.

The Emotion Decoder Ring: Translating Tween Communication

Imagine having a secret decoder for tween emotions – where "I'm fine" actually translates to "I'm drowning in feelings but don't possess the vocabulary to explain what's happening," and complete silence signals "I need you desperately but haven't figured out how to bridge this emotional gap without losing my dignity."

Welcome to the mysterious world of tween emotional communication, where nothing means what it appears to mean on the surface, and every conversation feels like attempting to solve cryptographic puzzles while riding a turbulent aircraft during electrical storms.

The sudden sob-fest is one of the most baffling mysteries of tween emotions, arriving with the surprise timing of a trapdoor in a perfectly normal day. Picture this scenario: calm morning, birds chirping optimistically, coffee brewing peacefully, everyone moving through everyday routines like civilized humans – then suddenly, *boom*: an emotional explosion over something as minor as the "wrong" breakfast bowl or a slightly tangled headphone cord.

These reactions aren't random acts of dramatic terrorism designed to test your sanity, though they certainly feel that way when you're trying to get everyone out the door on time. They're the result of hormonal surges running wild, brain development that resembles construction zones with inadequate safety protocols, and accumulated stress from sources you might not even recognize as stressful.

Hormonal fluctuations affect tween brains like puppet masters who've had too much caffeine and questionable judgment about timing. Estrogen and testosterone don't just influence physical development – they also affect neurotransmitters tied to mood regulation, impulse control, and emotional intensity, creating internal experiences that can feel overwhelming even to adults who know what's happening.

Meanwhile, the prefrontal cortex, responsible for logical thinking and emotional regulation, lags significantly behind the amygdala, which processes emotions and kicks off fight-or-flight responses with the enthusiasm of overzealous security guards. This biological reality means your tween experiences adult-sized emotions with child-sized coping mechanisms, creating perfect conditions for dramatic reactions to seemingly minor sparks – as if their internal alarm system is set to "toast is burning" levels of urgency.

When she sobs over a broken pencil, or he melts down because his favorite shirt is in the laundry, they're not being unreasonable or manipulative – they're managing overwhelming feelings with limited emotional tools while their brains undergo a major renovation… and someone definitely forgot to post the "Pardon Our Dust" sign.

Noticing what sets these moments off helps you respond wisely instead of taking it personally or assuming it reflects your parenting failures. Common catalysts include hunger that turns mild frustration into an existential crisis ("I'm starving" after eating 14 minutes ago), fatigue that makes standard challenges feel impossible, social stress that cranks everything up to "pressure cooker," and even positive excitement that becomes too much when it overloads their processing capacity – like trying to run ten apps at once on a phone with 3% battery.

The Tantrum Evolution: From Whimper to Nuclear Meltdown

Understanding how emotional meltdowns escalate helps you intervene effectively at each stage rather than waiting until you need a hazmat team to handle the emotional fallout. The progression follows predictable patterns, even when the content seems to defy all logical explanation.

The whimper stage often begins with subtle signs that require detective skills to spot – slightly glassy eyes that hint at a meltdown loading, heavy sighs that could power a small generator, or a lower lip tremble that signals the emotional pressure gauge is creeping into the red.

At this stage, gentle check-ins and small comfort offerings can often prevent escalation into more dramatic territory. Sometimes they just need acknowledgment that something feels difficult, along with minor adjustments like favorite snacks that possess mysterious mood-stabilizing properties or cozy blankets that apparently contain therapeutic powers.

During the crying crescendo, tears begin to flow, words become increasingly unclear, and emotional intensity rises to levels that would register on seismic equipment. This stage benefits from physical comfort if they're receptive – sitting beside them like emotional bodyguards, offering hugs that communicate unconditional love, or simply staying calm and present. At the same time, they process whatever the catalyst was for the emotional response.

Avoid trying to solve problems or offer brilliant advice during this phase, because their emotional processing systems are too overwhelmed to handle logical input. They need emotional support more than practical solutions, like having someone hold their hand during turbulence rather than explaining aerodynamic principles.

The screaming sonata represents peak emotional intensity, in which logic has completely vacated the premises, and their voice reaches frequencies previously thought to exist only in dog whistles and smoke alarms. Your primary job at this stage is to ensure everyone's safety while resisting the temptation to match their intensity with your own escalated responses.

Speaking softly creates contrast that often helps them begin de-escalating naturally, like providing calm eye-of-the-storm energy that demonstrates emotional regulation in real time. Think of yourself as an emotional lighthouse providing steady guidance during navigational challenges.

The exhausted collapse follows peak intensity as emotional storms burn themselves out, leaving your tween drained, confused, and often embarrassed about their dramatic display of feelings. This recovery period requires gentle reentry support – offering water since crying is genuinely dehydrating, providing quiet presence without pressure to discuss everything immediately, and eventually helping them process what happened once they're emotionally ready.

Throughout this entire cycle, remember that emotional intensity feels completely real and overwhelming to them, regardless of how trivial the spark might seem from an adult perspective. Your calm, consistent presence teaches them that emotions are manageable, temporary, and don't threaten fundamental safety or family relationships.

Friendship Fiascos: Surviving the Social Meltdowns

We covered the mechanics of tween friendship dynamics in Chapter 3 – the group chats, the mean girl tactics, the exclusion games. This section is about what happens when that drama lands in your living room as a sobbing, inconsolable mess.

Friendship pain has a specific quality that parents often underestimate. When your tween announces that their best friend "hates them now," they're not being dramatic – they're experiencing genuine grief. The intensity can feel like an adult breakup, except they don't yet have the life experience that whispers, "This is awful... and you will survive it."

Friendship problems don't always arrive as obvious meltdowns. Watch for sudden phone-checking anxiety, mood crashes after social media scrolling, vague answers about lunch ("I just sat with some people"), or declining invitations to events they'd normally attend. Sometimes the silence tells you more than the sobbing. Physical symptoms often accompany social stress – stomachaches before school, headaches that appear on Sunday evenings, or sleep disruption that coincides with friendship turbulence. Their bodies process social pain as real pain because, neurologically speaking, it is.

When the meltdown arrives, your instinct will be to fix, minimize, or explain. Resist all three. Avoid responses like "You'll make new friends," "She wasn't a real friend anyway," "This won't matter in five years," or "Have you tried just talking to her?" Try instead: "That sounds really painful." "Tell me what happened." "I'm here." Then stop talking and let them fill the space. The urge to immediately fix the situation or explain why these friends aren't worthy of their loyalty comes from love, but it short-circuits their processing. They need to feel the pain before they can move through it, and they need you to witness that pain without rushing them past it.

Expect stages similar to other grief: shock ("I can't believe she did that"), anger ("I hate her"), bargaining ("Maybe if I apologize for nothing she'll talk to me again"), sadness ("Nobody likes me"), and eventually acceptance ("I guess we're just not as close anymore"). These stages may cycle within an hour or span weeks. Don't be surprised when they loop back to anger after you thought they'd reached acceptance, or when sadness resurfaces unexpectedly weeks later. Grief isn't linear, and grief from friendship follows the same messy path as any other loss.

Normal friendship pain, while intense, eventually shifts. Concerning patterns include social withdrawal that extends beyond a specific friendship, statements about being fundamentally unlikable or worthless, persistent physical symptoms, or using friendship drama to avoid all social situations. These patterns suggest the friendship issue might be masking anxiety, depression, or self-esteem struggles that need deeper attention. If friendship pain seems to confirm beliefs they already held about their own worthlessness, that's a signal to seek additional support.

Your job isn't to fix this friendship or prevent future pain – it's to be the safe place they land when social life gets hard. Every friendship crisis they survive with your steady support teaches them that relationships can hurt without destroying them, that they can recover from rejection, and that their worth isn't determined by who sat with them at lunch. These relationships feel intensely important because they're practicing what they'll need for adult relationships – navigating conflict, disappointment, forgiveness, and boundary-setting through real-world experience. Your calm presence during the chaos is the curriculum.

Crush Confusion: Love's Emotional Tornado

First crushes arrive with all the subtlety of natural disasters, creating emotional upheaval that affects every aspect of daily life while remaining largely invisible to outside observers who can't understand why homework suddenly seems impossible. Appetite disappears completely without an apparent medical cause.

Early signs of a crush can resemble medical conditions that require parental awareness and gentle management, while balancing support with realistic expectations. Sudden obsession with appearance, mysterious stomach flutters, social media deep-dives into someone's posting history from three years ago, and dramatic mood swings based on whether their crush made eye contact today – congratulations, romance has entered the building.

When crushes develop, normal priorities reorganize around opportunities to interact with the object of affection in ways that would fascinate behavioral psychologists. Math homework becomes "negotiable" while doodling their name in notebook margins takes on urgent importance that somehow outranks academic responsibilities. Family conversations fade into background noise while every text notification sparks hope that, possibly, it's a message from their special person.

The transformation affects their entire personality in ways that can be both endearing and concerning. They might suddenly develop an interest in activities they've never mentioned before because their crush enjoys them, or change their appearance preferences to match what they think might be appealing to someone else.

Heartbreak during this developmental stage feels genuinely devastating because they're experiencing these intense emotions for the first time without context for how temporary romantic feelings can be or understanding that rejection doesn't reflect personal inadequacy. When their crush chooses someone else, shows no interest, or simply remains oblivious to their existence, the emotional pain mirrors adult heartbreak in intensity, but lacks the perspective that comes from surviving previous romantic disappointments.

Supporting them through crush experiences requires validation without minimization, because dismissing their feelings as "puppy love" or temporary infatuation invalidates real emotional experiences that feel earth-shaking to them. When they declare that their life is over because their crush said they're "like a sister," resist the urge to explain why this represents dodged bullets or a better opportunity ahead.

Instead, acknowledge that rejection genuinely hurts, and provide comfort and perspective appropriate to their developmental stage. Sometimes they need time to process disappointment before they're ready for encouraging words about future possibilities or reminders about their intrinsic worth.

Teaching healthy crush behaviors is essential, as these experiences establish patterns for future romantic relationships that can influence dating approaches throughout adolescence and into adulthood. Help them understand the difference between normal interest and obsessive behavior, appropriate ways to express attraction, and how to handle rejection gracefully while keeping self-respect—and respect for others—intact.

Self-Esteem Battles: The Internal War Zone

The mirror becomes both an ally and an enemy during tweendom as your child forms a shifting relationship with their changing appearance and evolving identity while navigating social pressures that can unsettle even the most confident adult.

Social media comparison is perhaps the most significant threat to healthy self-esteem development among modern tweens, providing endless opportunities to compare their real, unfiltered daily lives with carefully curated, edited highlight reels from others. This constant comparison creates impossible standards that leave even confident children feeling inadequate about ordinary human experiences.

Instagram, TikTok, and Snapchat provide constant exposure to content that appears effortless, yet it often requires advanced editing, perfect lighting, and multiple attempts to achieve the desired results. When your tween compares their morning appearance to influencers who've spent hours preparing for single photos, the comparison feels personal rather than recognizing the production value involved.

Combating comparison culture requires active intervention rather than hoping they'll develop immunity on their own through osmosis. Teaching them to identify photo-editing and filter effects, showing them the behind-the-scenes reality of social media content creation, and helping them curate feeds that emphasize diverse body types, authentic content, and positive messaging rather than perfectionist performances are essential parental responsibilities.

Building authentic self-worth involves expanding one's identity beyond physical appearance to include character traits, abilities, achievements, and contributions to family and community that reflect one's actual value as a person. Instead of focusing exclusively on appearance, celebrate their kindness toward friends, acknowledge their creative projects, recognize their academic efforts, and emphasize the many ways they add value to their communities.

Body image challenges intensify during physical development as they adjust to changing proportions, new sensations, and social responses to their evolving appearance that can feel beyond their control. Helping them develop body neutrality – acceptance and appreciation of what their bodies can do, rather than constant evaluation of how they look compared to impossible standards – lays a foundation for lifelong healthy relationships with their physical selves.

Teaching media literacy helps them critically evaluate messages about beauty, success, and self-worth that bombard them daily through advertising, entertainment, and social media, designed to create insecurity that drives consumer behavior. When they understand how these messages are constructed and why companies benefit from making people feel inadequate, they develop immunity to manipulation tactics.

Crisis Recognition: When to Call the Emotional Emergency Squad

Everything we've discussed so far falls within the range of normal tween emotional development – intense, sometimes exhausting, but ultimately healthy growing pains. However, some situations require more than parental patience and chocolate. Knowing the difference matters.

Sometimes intense emotions go beyond what parents can reasonably handle at home and move into territory where outside support is the safest, healthiest step – for both their immediate well-being and long-term emotional growth. Recognizing these moments helps you respond with the right resources rather than simply hoping the concerning behaviors fade on their own.

Mental health emergencies require immediate expert attention rather than family intervention alone. Any mention of self-harm, expressions of wanting to disappear or not be alive, dangerous risk-taking behaviors that seem designed to cause injury, or substance experimentation signals the need for evaluation and support from trained specialists in adolescent mental health.

Persistent patterns that continue for more than two weeks without improvement suggest underlying issues that benefit from experienced guidance rather than continued family management alone. Complete social withdrawal from all activities and relationships, dramatic academic performance changes that don't respond to support interventions, sleep disruption that affects daily functioning despite good sleep hygiene, or extreme mood variations that interfere with everyday activities warrant consultation with a trained therapist or counselor.

Eating disorder warning signs often develop during this period as body image concerns intersect with control issues and social pressures that create perfect storms for unhealthy relationships with food and exercise. Dramatic changes in eating patterns, obsessive exercise behaviors that consume increasing amounts of time, constant body criticism that doesn't respond to reassurance, or secretive behaviors around food require an evaluation from specialists familiar with adolescent development.

Finding appropriate help involves understanding different types of support available and matching services to your child's specific needs while navigating insurance requirements and availability in your geographic area. Pediatricians provide medical evaluations and referrals; school counselors offer immediate support and academic coordination; licensed therapists provide ongoing emotional skill development, and psychiatrists evaluate medication needs when other interventions are insufficient.

Preparing your tween for this requires framing therapy as skill-building rather than punishment or evidence of personal failure, because their attitude toward seeking help influences treatment effectiveness. Emphasize that asking for support demonstrates strength and wisdom; allow them to participate in choosing their therapist when possible; and prepare for initial resistance as normal rather than evidence that help isn't needed.

Surviving the Emotional Weather Systems

You've now developed essential skills for emotional meteorology – reading storm systems that change faster than actual weather, keeping your own calm while theirs falls apart, recognizing when help is needed, and helping your tween build emotional capacity that will serve them throughout life.

Remember that emotional intensity during tweendom reflects normal, healthy development rather than personal failing or inadequate parenting, even when daily life feels like managing a natural disaster. Your tween is learning to manage adult-sized feelings as they develop emotional regulation, making patience and understanding essential components of your support strategy.

Every emotional storm you move through together builds resilience, trust, and communication skills that strengthen your relationship and prepare your child for adult emotional challenges that will require these same coping strategies. Your steady presence during their most turbulent moments teaches them that emotions are temporary, manageable, and don't threaten fundamental safety or love.

The young person standing in your living room, cycling through emotions with impressive speed and intensity while creating household drama worthy of an Emmy nomination, is developing the emotional intelligence they'll need as adults. Trust the process, maintain your sense of humor, and remember that this phase is building character for both of you while providing excellent training for crisis know-how.

Keep your candy supply well-stocked, your sense of humor intact, and your expectations realistic about emotional stability during this developmental phase. You're not just surviving daily drama – you're teaching someone to navigate the complicated world of human emotions with grace, resilience, and ideally a sense of humor about the beautiful chaos of growing up.

five

the digital playground & tween slang 101

If you think texting is just "type a few words, hit send," you haven't experienced tween communication. They've created an entirely new language – part acronym, part emoji, part telepathic understanding that somehow bypasses traditional grammar. Your mission, should you choose to accept it (and really, do you have a choice?), is to decode this linguistic maze while making sure your sanity stays intact.

Cracking the Code: When "LOL" Doesn't Mean Laughing

Disclaimer: When I wrote this chapter, 'slay' and 'fire' were still current. By the time you read this, my tweens have probably informed me that these words are now 'cheugy' (which itself might be now outdated). The cycle continues.

Let's say your tween sends you a message that reads "OMG Mom periodt that's so cap fr fr 💀 " and expects you to respond appropriately. Meanwhile, you're staring at your phone like it's written in ancient hieroglyphics, wondering when you became the digital equivalent of your grandmother trying to program a VCR.

The truth is, tween slang isn't just random gibberish designed to confuse parents (though that's certainly a bonus feature). It's actually a sophisticated communication system that enables them to express mixed emotions, establish social bonds, and navigate a rapidly changing world. Understanding this language isn't about becoming fluent overnight – it's about showing respect for their culture and keeping a connection across the generational divide.

Let's start with the basics. When your tween says something is "fire," they're not reporting a household emergency – they're giving you the highest possible compliment. That new song you played in the car? Fire. The dinner you made last Tuesday? Apparently, also fire (who knew your lasagna had such street cred?). On the flip side, if something is "mid," it's painfully mediocre, like lukewarm coffee or a movie that's trying too hard to be cool.

The word "slay" has evolved far beyond its medieval origins. When your daughter announces she's going to "slay" her presentation, she's channeling her inner confidence warrior, preparing to absolutely crush it. And if someone is described as "the GOAT," they're not being compared to barnyard animals – they're the Greatest of All Time, worthy of serious respect.

But here's where it gets tricky: context is everything. "That's so sus" could mean anything from "that excuse sounds fishy" to "I don't trust that new kid's vibe." The exact phrase can carry different emotional weight depending on the tone, timing, and who's saying it. It's like learning a language where the dictionary rewrites itself every few months.

The Great Emoji Evolution

Remember when a smiley face was just a smiley face? Those were simpler times. Today's emoji communication requires a PhD in digital anthropology. The skull emoji (💀) doesn't indicate death threats – it means they're "dying" of laughter. The cap emoji (🧢) isn't about hats—it's how they call something fake or say "that's a lie." And that innocent-looking pleading face (🥺) is emotional warfare disguised as cuteness, deployed when they want something desperately.

Your tween has likely mastered the art of emoji storytelling, crafting entire narratives using nothing but tiny pictures. They can convey the epic saga of their Monday morning using a coffee cup, a crying face, and a rainbow, somehow communicating that they spilled coffee on their homework, but their friend helped them fix it, and now everything's okay. Meanwhile, you're still figuring out whether the thumbs-up emoji makes you look supportive or passive-aggressive.

The evolution continues with reaction emojis and custom responses. Your family group chat has probably become a testing ground for increasingly creative emoji combinations, where your simple "see you at dinner" gets responses ranging from a single heart to a parade of dancing hamburgers. Embrace the chaos. Your confused responses often become family legend, quoted for years to come.

The Bermuda Triangle of Time

Once upon a time, parents worried about television rotting children's brains. Now we have TikTok, which has somehow convinced an entire generation that learning elaborate dance routines is a completely reasonable use of three hours – and honestly, after watching your tween nail a particularly complicated one, you might start to agree.

TikTok operates on its own logic system. Videos longer than thirty seconds are considered feature films. Trends appear and disappear faster than mayflies. Your tween can spend three hours watching people make miniature food or explaining why pineapple belongs on pizza, emerging from this digital rabbit hole with strong opinions about topics they'd never considered before.

The algorithm is particularly devious. It learns your tween's preferences better than you know their favorite color, serving up content perfectly calibrated to keep them scrolling. One minute, they're watching skateboarding fails, the next they're deeply invested in someone's grandmother's cooking tips, followed immediately by a philosophical discussion about whether cereal is soup. It's like having a personalized television channel that never stops broadcasting exactly what they didn't know they wanted to see.

As a parent, you're caught between appreciating the creativity and education happening on the platform (some of these kids are genuinely talented) and worrying about the endless scroll trap. The key is establishing boundaries without declaring total war. Screen time limits require more back-and-forth than buying a house. "Just one more video" becomes the new "five more minutes" of childhood bargaining.

YouTube: The Other Screen Time

While TikTok gets most of the parental attention, YouTube remains a massive presence in tween digital life – and it operates quite differently. Where TikTok serves bite-sized content designed for endless scrolling, YouTube offers longer-form videos that your tween might watch with surprising focus. The same kid who can't sit through a thirty-minute TV show will happily watch a forty-five-minute video essay about the history of a video game or a two-hour livestream of their favorite creator playing Minecraft.

YouTube rabbit holes are a phenomenon in themselves. Your tween starts watching a tutorial on how to beat a difficult game level, which leads to a video about gaming strategies, which leads to a documentary about the game's development, which somehow ends at a video about Japanese work culture at 11 PM on a school night. The algorithm is designed to keep serving content, and the longer format means each video consumes more time than a TikTok scroll session, even if it feels more purposeful.

The content itself ranges from genuinely educational to completely mindless – often within the same creator's channel. Your tween might learn fascinating things about history, science, or creative skills from YouTube, then follow it up with an hour of watching someone open mystery boxes or react to other people's videos. Trying to categorize YouTube as "good" or "bad" screen time misses the point; it's a platform that hosts everything, and your tween's consumption will be equally varied.

Unlike TikTok's rapid-fire format, YouTube creates deeper engagement with specific creators. Your tween might follow certain YouTubers for years, watching them grow and change and feeling a genuine investment in their lives and content. This sustained attention creates stronger parasocial bonds than shorter-form content, which brings us to a phenomenon worth understanding.

Snapchat Stories and the Art of Temporary Drama

Snapchat introduced the revolutionary concept of messages disappearing, which seemed brilliant until you realized it just encouraged more reckless communication. Your tween now lives in a world where embarrassing photos vanish after ten seconds, but screenshots are forever, creating a fascinating tension between temporary confidence and permanent consequences.

The Snapchat streak has become a relationship status indicator more significant than anniversary dates. Missing a streak after 200 days is considered a personal tragedy that requires emergency intervention. Your tween will wake up in a panic at midnight, realizing they forgot to send their daily streak photo, desperately trying to salvage digital relationships through blurry selfies taken in bathroom mirrors.

Stories add a new dimension. These twenty-four-hour glimpses into daily life require careful curation. Your tween becomes a documentary filmmaker of their own existence, choosing which moments deserve public consumption. The process of selecting the perfect breakfast story requires more consideration than most adults give to major life decisions.

GAMING Culture and the World of Discord

If your tween – especially if you're raising a boy – spends hours with a headset on, talking to the screen while mashing controller buttons, you're witnessing the social hub that gaming has become. This isn't the solitary activity it might appear to be. For many tweens, gaming is where friendships form, social skills develop, and a significant portion of their social life unfolds.

Discord has become the digital living room where gaming social life unfolds. Initially built for gamers to coordinate during play, it's evolved into a platform where tweens join servers based on shared interests – favorite games, music, YouTubers, or just friend groups from school. Each server functions like a mini social network with its own culture, rules, and social dynamics. Your tween might belong to a dozen servers, each with its own expectations – and each inviting a slight variation of who they are.

Voice chat creates a unique social environment that falls between texting and in-person conversation. Your tween might spend hours in voice channels with friends, sometimes actively gaming together and sometimes just hanging out while everyone does their own thing – the digital equivalent of being in the same room without necessarily interacting. This ambient friendship feels strange to parents who grew up with phone calls that had clear beginnings and endings, but for tweens, it's a natural way to maintain connection.

Gaming communities come with their own social hierarchies that your tween is learning to navigate. Skill level matters – being good at a game earns respect – but so does knowledge, humor, and social savvy. Server moderators hold power. Established members have status that newcomers have to earn. Your tween is learning about social structures, reputation building, and community norms in ways that will translate to future workplaces and social groups, even if it looks like they're just playing video games.

Online friendships with people they've never met in person deserve acknowledgment rather than dismissal. Your tween might have genuine, meaningful friendships with gaming buddies who live across the country or around the world. They've collaborated on challenges, celebrated victories, supported each other through difficult days, and developed genuine affection – all without ever being in the same room. These relationships are authentic even if they don't look like the friendships you had growing up.

That said, online friendships call for their own safety conversations – separate from the ones you'd have about in-person friends. Your tween should understand that people online might not be who they claim to be, that personal information should be guarded, and that any adult who wants to keep their friendship secret from parents is a red flag. These conversations work better as ongoing dialogue than as one-time lectures, and they're more effective when you approach them with curiosity about their online world rather than suspicion.

Ask your tween about their gaming friends. Learn their usernames, understand the games they play together, and show genuine interest in the social world they've built. You might be surprised by the depth of these relationships and the social intelligence your tween is developing, while you thought they were just staring at a screen.

Digital Drama and Online Safety

The internet has given tween drama new tools, new audiences, and new permanence. Understanding how these digital mechanics work helps you recognize what your tween is navigating and have informed conversations about online behavior – both as targets and participants.

Screenshots have fundamentally changed the stakes of digital communication. That "disappearing" Snapchat message? Someone can capture it in a fraction of a second. That rant your tween sent to a trusted friend? It can be forwarded to the entire grade before lunch ends. The permanence of screenshots means that moments of anger, vulnerability, or poor judgment can follow your tween long after they've moved on emotionally. Teaching them to assume anything they send could become public isn't paranoia – it's digital literacy.

Group chat dynamics have become a primary arena for social maneuvering. Creating a new group chat that excludes one person from the friend group sends a clear message without anyone having to say anything directly. Removing someone from an existing chat is even more pointed. Your tween might find themselves suddenly unable to access conversations they were part of yesterday, or notice a new chat has formed with everyone except them. The silence communicates everything.

"Left on read" has become a social weapon with surprising power. When your tween sees that someone opened their message but chose not to respond, the silence feels intentional in a way that pre-digital communication never allowed. Before read receipts, you could assume someone was busy. Now, being left on read communicates deliberate dismissal – or at least that's how it feels. Some tweens deliberately weaponize this, leaving messages unanswered as a power move or a form of punishment.

Vague posting and subtweets enable public drama without direct confrontation. Posting "Some people are so fake" or "Love when my 'friends' talk behind my back" lets everyone know something happened without naming names – though usually the target and the audience know exactly who's being referenced. This creates drama that's deniable ("I wasn't talking about YOU") while still causing damage. The ambiguity is the point: it generates attention, invites inquiry, and puts the target in the position of either ignoring it or looking defensive by responding.

Strategic posting uses photos and stories as social currency. Posting pictures from a hangout everyone wasn't invited to, tagging some friends but not others, or timing posts to coincide with events your tween was excluded from – these are all ways drama plays out through what appears to be innocent content sharing. Your tween might struggle to articulate why a particular post upset them, even though "nothing mean was said." The cruelty is in the curation.

Digital footprints extend far beyond immediate social circles. What your tween posts today could resurface during college applications, job interviews, or future relationships. This isn't about scaring them into digital silence – it's about helping them understand that their online presence is cumulative. Screenshots from middle school drama have appeared in high school conflicts years later. Teaching thoughtful posting habits now protects their future selves.

Privacy settings offer protection but require ongoing attention. Platforms change their defaults regularly, new features launch with public settings, and your tween might not realize their content is visible beyond their intended audience. Regular privacy audits – checking who can see posts, who can message them, and what information is public – should become routine digital hygiene. But also help them understand that privacy settings aren't foolproof: anything shared digitally can potentially be shared further.

Teaching digital citizenship means addressing both sides of these mechanics. Your tween needs to recognize when these tactics are being used against them, but they also need to understand when they're participating in digital cruelty themselves – sometimes without realizing it. Screenshotting a friend's embarrassing message to share with others, leaving someone on read as punishment, or creating exclusive group chats might feel like normal social behavior because "everyone does it." Helping them see these actions from the receiving end builds empathy that translates into kinder online behavior.

For guidance on supporting your tween through the emotional fallout of digital drama, see the section on friendship dynamics in Chapter 3 and the guidance on friendship meltdowns in Chapter 4.

WHEN DIGITAL WORLDS Collide with Real Life

Perhaps the most challenging aspect of parenting digital natives is helping them balance their online and offline experiences. Your tween might have friends they've never met in person but feel incredibly close to, relationships that exist primarily through shared gaming experiences or social media interactions. These connections can be meaningful and valuable, but they also lack the full context of in-person relationships.

The pressure to maintain an online persona can be exhausting. Your tween might spend significant energy crafting the perfect image for their social media presence, carefully choosing photos that make their life look interesting and enviable. This performance of happiness and success can become overwhelming, especially when they're struggling with normal tween challenges like insecurity, friendship drama, or academic pressure.

Screen time battles become power struggles over control, independence, and values. Your tween sees digital connection as essential to their social survival, while you worry about everything from sleep deprivation to missing real-world experiences. The solution usually involves compromise, clear expectations, and understanding that technology isn't inherently evil – it's a tool that can be used well or poorly.

Your tween might talk about a YouTuber, streamer, or influencer with the familiarity usually reserved for close friends. They know this person's pet's name, their coffee order, their relationship history, and their opinions on everything from skin care products to pizza toppings. They feel genuine emotion when this creator shares good news or struggles. But this person has no idea your tween exists.

This is a parasocial relationship – a one-sided emotional connection to someone who doesn't know you personally. It's not new (people had parasocial relationships with movie stars and TV personalities for decades), but the intimacy of modern content creation makes these bonds feel closer than ever. When a YouTuber films in their bedroom, shares daily life updates, and responds to comments, the relationship feels more mutual than it actually is.

These relationships aren't inherently unhealthy. They can provide comfort, inspiration, and a sense of connection, especially for tweens who feel isolated or like they don't quite fit in. Following a creator who shares their identity or interests can help your tween feel less alone. Watching someone they admire navigate challenges can model resilience and problem-solving. The emotional investment is real, and dismissing it as "just someone on the internet" misses what your tween is getting from the relationship.

Concern becomes appropriate when parasocial relationships replace, rather than supplement, real-world connections; when your tween's sense of self-worth becomes tied to a creator's content or acknowledgment; or when they're spending money they don't have on subscriptions, merchandise, or donations, hoping for recognition. If your tween seems to have more emotional investment in a stranger's life than in their own friendships and activities, that's worth exploring – not with judgment, but with curiosity about what needs that relationship is meeting.

Approach these relationships with the same interest you'd show in their real-world friendships. Ask about the creators they follow. Watch a video with them and ask what they enjoy about this person's content. Understanding why certain creators resonate with your tween gives you insight into their values, interests, and the kind of person they're becoming – even if the relationship only flows one direction.

Building Digital Literacy Together

Rather than positioning yourself as the digital police, consider becoming a curious student of your tween's online world. Ask them to teach you about platforms they enjoy, not to spy or judge, but to understand what they find engaging genuinely. This approach builds connection while giving you insight into their interests and social dynamics.

Discuss digital footprints and future implications without resorting to scare tactics. Help them understand that their online presence will likely outlast their tween years, and that cultivating a positive digital reputation serves their long-term interests. This doesn't mean they can't make mistakes or have fun – it means encouraging thoughtful choices about what they share and how they interact online.

Model healthy digital habits yourself. If you want them to put away their devices during family time, you need to do the same. If you want them to think critically about online information, demonstrate fact-checking and source evaluation in your own digital consumption. Children learn more from observing our behavior than from listening to our lectures.

The Evolving Language of Connection

Ultimately, tween slang and digital communication serve the same purpose as any language – connecting with others and expressing identity. When your tween uses current slang or communicates primarily through memes, they're participating in their peer culture and establishing their place in their social world. Your job isn't to translate every word or approve every platform – it's to stay connected enough to understand their world while helping them navigate it safely.

The specific words and platforms will continue changing. By the time you master current slang, it will probably be outdated. What remains constant is the underlying need for connection, understanding, and guidance as they learn to communicate effectively and kindly in an increasingly connected world.

Keep asking questions, stay curious about their interests, and remember that every generation develops its own communication style. Your parents probably didn't understand your slang either, and somehow you all survived. The goal isn't perfect comprehension – it's sustaining a relationship and providing guidance as they develop their own digital voice.

Staying Connected Across the Digital Divide

You've survived the crash course in digital tween culture, from decoding mysterious acronyms to understanding why thirty-second videos can hold their attention for hours. The landscape will continue to evolve, new platforms will emerge, and the slang will continue to change. Still, your role remains consistent – providing guidance, maintaining connection, and helping your tween develop healthy relationships with technology.

Remember that behind all the digital communication and ever-changing slang is still your child, trying to figure out their place in the world and maintain connections with friends. The medium may differ from your childhood, but the fundamental human needs for belonging, understanding, and expression remain the same.

six
out of the mouths of tweens: unfiltered commentary on life

Somewhere along the way, your tween becomes both a comedic prodigy and a walking improv show—often at the same time. They exist in that in-between space where childhood innocence meets emerging sophistication, and it's a perfect breeding ground for comments that range from accidentally profound to intentionally savage.

The beauty of tween humor lies in its complete authenticity. They haven't yet learned to filter their observations through adult politeness or social conventions, which means their commentary on life, family, and the general absurdity of existence arrives unvarnished and surprisingly insightful. Sometimes they're trying to be funny; other times they're making innocent observations that happen to land like perfectly crafted comedy.

Generational Roasts: When Kids Become Comedy Critics

Nothing prepares you for the moment your offspring transforms into a comedy critic with devastating accuracy about your technological limitations and cultural references. These generational observations arrive at a timing that stand-up comedians would envy and with accuracy that cuts straight to the heart of your attempts to stay relevant.

Technology commentary represents their most fertile ground for material. When I asked Bash to help me connect to Bluetooth, he took my phone, fixed it in four seconds, and handed it back with the observation, 'You always make it harder than it is.' He's nine. He's not wrong.

Their observations about our attempts to understand their world often reveal truths we'd prefer to ignore. After watching Sim attempt a trending dance, Mara offered genuinely helpful feedback: 'Dad, you're doing all the right moves, just... not at the right times. Or speeds.' She was trying to be nice about it.

Music and entertainment preferences become frequent targets of cultural commentary. Mara has developed a polite way of critiquing my music: 'It's not bad, it's just... old-sounding.' When I pointed out that it was recorded before she was born, she nodded as if that explained everything.

The most cutting observations often focus on our attempts to use their language or participate in their cultural references. When Sim tried to call dinner 'bussin,' both kids went silent. Bash looked at Mara. Mara looked at Bash. Some kind of sibling telepathy occurred. Finally, Mara spoke for both of them: 'Dad, you can just say it's good.'

Accidental Philosophy: Deep Thoughts from Developing Minds

Perhaps the most surprising aspect of tween communication is their talent for philosophical observation — worthy of a professor — paired with the fresh perspective of minds still forming their understanding of how the world operates.

Existential observations emerge from their daily experiences with startling regularity. Bash once asked why he had to redo a worksheet he got wrong. I explained that's how you learn. He considered this and said, 'So I got it wrong, which means I learned, but now I'm in trouble for learning?' I told him just to do the worksheet.

Scientific curiosity combines with literal thinking to produce questions that challenge assumptions adults take for granted. At bedtime, Bash asked why we get tired at night. I explained that our bodies need rest. He thought about it and said, 'But my body doesn't know what time it is. It doesn't have a phone.' He had a point.

Social dynamics provide rich material for their philosophical musings. At a family party, Bash asked me why Auntie asked how school was going, but walked away while he was still answering. 'Did I talk too long, or did she not actually want to know?' I told him that some questions are just for politeness. He frowned. 'That seems like a waste of a question.'

Their relationship with technology often produces insights that feel both naive and profound. During a streaming outage, Mara said, 'It's weird how when the internet doesn't work, there's nothing to do, but before the internet existed, people had stuff to do all the time.' She paused. 'What did they do?' I told her they went outside. She did not go outside.

Questions about fairness and justice frequently reveal thinking that cuts through adult rationalizations to core principles. When I told Mara her screen time was up, she pointed out that I'd been on my phone for the last hour. 'So screen time is bad for kids but not for adults?' I explained that I was responding to work emails. She asked if I could prove it. I could not.

Unfiltered Honesty: Truth Bombs Disguised as Innocent Comments

Tween honesty operates without any filters that adults develop over years of social conditioning, resulting in observations that are simultaneously brutal and refreshingly authentic. Their comments cut straight to the truth without consideration for whether that truth might be uncomfortable to receive.

Appearance commentary lands with forensic accuracy and absolutely no filter. When I came downstairs dressed for a work event, Mara looked me over and said, 'You look nice. Different, but nice.' When I asked what she meant by different, she said, 'Like you're trying harder than usual.' She thought this was a compliment.

Cooking critiques often demonstrate their capacity to deliver constructive feedback with devastating directness. When I served a new casserole, both kids were quiet for a suspiciously long time. Finally, Bash asked, 'Is there more of the regular dinner, or just this?' Mara added, 'We're not saying it's bad. We're just saying we're not hungry.' The casserole was not made again.

Fashion observations often reflect their developing aesthetic sense, combined with complete disregard for tactful communication. Before a parent-teacher conference, I asked Mara how I looked. She studied me and said, 'You look like a mom.' I wondered if that was bad. 'No, it's just... accurate.' She returned to her phone, case apparently closed.

Behavioral commentary reveals their keen observation skills and growing understanding of adult psychology. Sim was assembling a desk and announced he was 'almost done' for the fourth time. Mara whispered to Bash, 'He's not almost done.' Bash whispered back, 'I know.' They'd learned to read the signs. They were correct – it took another two hours.

Their assessments of family dynamics often provide insights that family therapists might envy. Comments like "Mom, you use cleaning as meditation, but angry meditation" or "Dad pretends to listen to music, but really he's just remembering when he was young" reveal a keen grasp of how adults process emotions and cope with life transitions.

Digital Native Wisdom: Technology Commentary from the Inside

Growing up as digital natives gives tweens a unique perspective on technology – one that often highlights how ridiculous adults look while trying to keep up.

When Mara tried to explain Instagram to her grandmother, she struggled to find the right words. Finally, she said, 'It's like a photo album, but you only put in pictures where you look good, and then you wait to see if people like them.' Grandma asked why you'd wait. Mara thought about it. 'I actually don't know.'

Autocorrect provides endless material. Bash was trying to text a friend and threw his phone down in frustration. 'My phone keeps changing what I say!' I told him it was trying to help. He looked at me with disbelief. 'It changed "haha" to "Hans." Who is Hans? Why does my phone think I know someone named Hans?'

Gaming commentary reveals just how much their view of achievement can differ. After Bash spent an hour trying to beat the same level, Sim suggested he take a break. Bash was horrified. 'I can't stop now, I almost had it.' He had not almost had it. He would try forty more times before dinner. When he finally won, he announced it to the household like he'd won an Olympic medal. In his mind, he had.

They are ruthless observers of our technology struggles. When Sim asked Mara to help him post something on Instagram, she watched him type with one finger and asked, 'Dad, why do you use your phone like it's hot?' He didn't have an answer. When I couldn't find an app on my phone, Bash took it from me, found it immediately, and handed it back without a word. The silence said everything.

Voice assistants bring out their best commentary. After listening to me argue with Alexa about the correct pronunciation of a song title, Mara observed, 'You know she's not real, right? You're fighting with a speaker.' Bash added, 'And losing.' They returned to their screens, enough said.

Even digital safety talks become material. When I reminded Bash about not talking to strangers online, he sighed heavily. 'Mom, I know. But also, strangers are more polite than the kids I actually know.' He had a point I wasn't prepared for.

Family Dynamics Through Fresh Eyes

Living within family systems while developing an independent perspective gives tweens unique vantage points for observing family patterns, traditions, and dynamics that adults might take for granted or miss entirely. Mara and Bash have become unofficial anthropologists of our household, documenting our quirks with the precision of researchers and the timing of comedians.

Sibling relationship commentary often reveals an understanding of family roles and dynamics that surprises parents with its accuracy. When I asked why Mara and Bash were arguing about who got the TV remote when neither of them was even watching TV, Mara shrugged and said, "We're not really fighting about the remote. We're fighting about who has to give in first." She was eleven. She'd already figured out what most adults learn in therapy.

Parent behavior analysis often yields insights that are uncomfortable to accept. During a particularly stressful week, Bash observed, "You and Dad keep having the same conversation but pretending it's about different things." When I asked what he meant, he said, "Like, you talk about the dishes, but you're really talking about something else. It's confusing." Sim and I exchanged a look. The kid was spot on.

Household routine observations often reveal how family systems function from the perspective of someone who participates but didn't design the systems. Mara once announced, "Our family runs on Dad's optimism and Mom's backup plans." Sim was delighted by this. I was... also not wrong. Bash added his own analysis: "Dad says yes first and thinks later. Mom thinks first and then says maybe." They've been studying us. They've drawn conclusions. The conclusions are accurate.

Holiday and tradition commentary provides a fresh perspective on family rituals that adults might approach automatically. Last Thanksgiving, while I was stressed about cooking timelines, table settings, and hosting over 40 friends and family, Bash asked, "Why do we spend more time getting ready for the fun part than actually having the fun part?" Before I could answer, Mara added, "But also, the getting-ready part is kind of fun too, so that could be the point?" I didn't have a response. They'd out-philosophied me while I was chopping onions.

Extended family dynamics often produce observations that reveal tweens' understanding of adult relationships and family history. After a visit from my mother, Mara noted, "Mimi still talks to you like you're learning how to be a grown-up." I said I'd always be her child, no matter how old I was. Mara considered this. "That's kind of sweet. But also, she reorganized your pantry, so she's probably right." Bash's contribution to the family analysis focused on Sim. 'Dad tells us stories about before he was a dad,' he said, 'because he wants us to know he used to be interesting.' Sim pretended to be offended. Bash patted his arm. 'You're still kind of interesting.' High praise. These kids see everything. They understand more than we give them credit for. And they're taking notes.

The Wisdom in Their Weirdness

Perhaps the most valuable aspect of tween commentary lies not in its intentional humor but in its capacity to reveal truths that adults might miss through familiarity, social conditioning, or simply being too close to situations to see them clearly.

Their questions about why things work the way they do often expose assumptions that deserve examination. When tweens ask why school days start so early if teenagers need more sleep, or why healthy food costs more than unhealthy food, or why adults ask for their opinions but then explain why those opinions are wrong, they're identifying genuine contradictions in systems that adults have learned to accept without question.

Observations of adult behavior often reveal patterns that could benefit from conscious attention. When tweens note that parents tell them not to interrupt but constantly interrupt each other, that adults preach patience while demonstrating impatience with technology, or that families value honesty but practice selective inclusion, they're providing valuable feedback on the consistency between stated values and actual behavior.

Their fresh perspective on social conventions often highlights arbitrary aspects of systems that adults take for granted. Questions about why certain clothes are considered appropriate for certain activities, why some emotions are acceptable in public while others aren't, or why politeness sometimes requires dishonesty reveal advanced thinking about social construction and cultural norms.

The combination of developing critical thinking skills and limited life experience creates a unique capacity to view situations without the weight of precedent or social expectation. When tweens observe that busy adults seem to have less fun than busy children, or that people spend money they don't have on things they don't need to impress people they don't like, they're often identifying truths that adult experience has obscured rather than clarified.

The Comedy of Growing Up

Recognition and appreciation of tween humor bridge generational perspectives and create shared experiences that strengthen family relationships. When parents can laugh with rather than at their children's observations, they validate both the humor and the thinking behind it.

Collecting and celebrating these moments of unintentional comedy creates family folklore that builds connection across time. Years later, families often recall and retell these observations as evidence of developing personalities, changing relationships, and a shared history that feels uniquely theirs.

Creating safe spaces for humor encourages tweens to continue sharing their observations and developing their communication skills. When families can laugh together about the absurdities of daily life, household stress, and generational differences, they build resilience that helps everyone navigate inevitable challenges with a better perspective.

The wit that emerges during this developmental stage often represents early evidence of adult personality traits and thinking patterns. Parents who pay attention to their tween's humor style – whether they gravitate toward observational comedy, wordplay, physical humor, or social satire – gain insights into how their child processes information and relates to the world. Your tween's observations about life, family, and the general absurdity of human existence provide more than entertainment – they offer windows into developing minds that are trying to make sense of a fast-changing, often confusing reality while still bringing a fresh perspective that can reveal truths adults have forgotten or learned to ignore.

These moments of unintentional wisdom and deliberate comedy represent your child's developing voice, growing confidence, and emerging ability to engage with the world through critical thinking and creative expression. When you appreciate their humor, you validate their perspective and encourage continued intellectual and emotional growth.

The young person making these observations is developing the communication skills, critical thinking abilities, and emotional intelligence they'll need as adults. Their capacity to find humor in challenging situations, spot contradictions in the systems around them, and maintain hope despite recognizing life's absurdities reflects emotional sophistication that will serve them well throughout their lives.

Keep collecting these moments, celebrating their insights, and remembering that sometimes the wisest observations come from minds that haven't yet learned what they're supposed to think impossible or inappropriate to notice.

seven
then vs. now: tweenhood 1990 vs. 2025

If parenting feels like you're using a roadmap from 1990 to navigate 2025 terrain, you're not imagining things. The landscape of tweenhood has transformed so dramatically that parents often feel like anthropologists studying a fascinating but alien culture that happens to live in their own homes. 1990 is my reference point – the year I turned eleven, right in the heart of my own tweenhood. But whether you grew up in the '80s, '90s, or even early 2000s, the contrast with today's tweenhood will feel familiar. The specific details change, but the sense of 'this is a whole new planet' remains.

Understanding these generational shifts isn't about nostalgia for "simpler times" or criticism of modern childhood – it's about building bridges between your experience and your child's reality. When you recognize how contrasting their world is from yours, you can respond to their challenges with empathy rather than confusion, and appreciate their adaptations rather than mourning changes you can't control.

The Information Revolution: From Encyclopedia Sets to Instant Everything

The most fundamental difference between 1990 and 2025 tweenhood involves access to information and entertainment.

This shift affects everything from how children learn to how they socialize, creating experiences that differ so dramatically from previous generations that they might as well be occurring on alternate planets.

In 1990, research required physical effort and planning. When tweens needed information for school projects, they hauled themselves to libraries, navigated card catalog systems that seemed designed by medieval librarians, and hoped their topic wasn't already claimed by other students who'd checked out the only relevant books. The microfiche machine lurked in library corners like an ancient artifact, requiring special skills and patience to extract any useful information from its mysterious depths.

This research process developed specific strengths that modern children rarely develop: patience with slow information gathering, comfort with incomplete data, and resourcefulness when preferred sources were unavailable. The limitation changed our relationship with knowledge itself. Information felt valuable because it required effort to obtain, and we learned to work with whatever we could find rather than expecting comprehensive, immediate answers to every question.

When I told Bash that I once spent an entire Saturday at the library researching dolphins for a school report, he asked, 'Why didn't you just Google it?' I explained that Google didn't exist. He stared at me like I'd said we used to communicate via smoke signals. 'So how did you find anything?' Buddy, that's the question that haunted my entire childhood.

Today's tweens inhabit an information ecosystem where Google provides instant answers to questions they haven't even finished formulating. When curiosity strikes about how tall giraffes are, whether dinosaurs had feathers, or why some people don't like cilantro, answers appear faster than they can type complete questions. This immediate access reshapes expectations about how quickly answers should appear and lowers tolerance for uncertainty or partial information.

This instant access cuts both ways. Modern tweens can dive deep into subjects that fascinate them, finding expert-level information and online communities that would have been impossible to discover in pre-Internet days. But they can also get impatient when answers don't appear immediately – and uneasy when answers are incomplete or uncertain.

Parents educated in the pre-Internet era often struggle to understand why their children seem unable to tolerate waiting for answers or working with limited information. What adults perceive as impatience is actually a normal adaptation to technological capabilities that provide instant gratification for intellectual curiosity.

Social Landscapes: From Neighborhood Networks to Global Connections

The geography of friendship has expanded from bicycle-riding distance to global reach, reshaping how tweens form relationships, maintain connections, and navigate social challenges.

In 1990, friendship circles were determined by physical proximity and shared activities. Children became friends with classmates, neighbors, and teammates because those were the people available for regular interaction. Social conflicts played out in limited spaces with finite audiences – playground drama stayed on the playground, and weekend recovery time provided natural breaks from social intensity.

These geographic limitations created certain advantages. Friendships often developed through shared physical experiences – building forts, exploring neighborhoods, participating in group activities that required coordination and compromise. Social instincts developed through face-to-face interaction, where children learned to read body language, navigate group dynamics, and resolve conflicts without adult mediation.

Modern tweens form friendships through shared interests rather than shared geography. They connect with people who enjoy the same games, music, or hobbies, regardless of location, creating communities of understanding that might not exist in their immediate physical environment. A child interested in obscure historical periods, specific art forms, or niche gaming communities can find peers who share their passion, rather than feeling isolated because of their unusual interests.

However, digital friendships also create new challenges. Online relationships lack the full context of in-person interaction, making it easier to misunderstand intentions or develop unrealistic expectations about digital friends. Conflict resolution becomes more challenging when hurt feelings lead to blocking, ghosting, or public drama that spreads beyond the original participants.

The social media amplification effect means that tween social challenges now have potentially larger audiences and longer lifespans. What might have been temporary playground drama in 1990 can become documented, shareable content that follows children across platforms and time periods.

Communication Evolution: From Landlines to Livestreams

The transformation of communication technology has revolutionized not just how tweens connect with others, but how they understand privacy, intimacy, and social boundaries. Communication in 1990 required planning and patience. Calling friends meant hoping they were home, navigating family landline politics, and accepting that conversations had audiences since cordless phones had limited range, so privacy meant stretching the cord as far as it would go and whispering. The scarcity made communication feel special – receiving calls or letters created excitement that modern children rarely experience around routine communication.

I tried to explain the concept of a busy signal to Mara. 'So you'd call someone, and if they were already on the phone, you'd just hear a beeping noise and have to try again later.' She looked horrified. 'You couldn't even leave a message?' No. 'Or text them?' No. 'What if it were an emergency?' We just... kept calling. She looked at me with genuine pity.

Letter writing, note passing, and even early email taught us to be more intentional with our words. When communication required effort, we thought more carefully about what we wanted to say. The delay between sending and receiving messages encouraged more careful composition, while the effort needed to maintain long-distance relationships meant that sustained connections represented genuine commitment.

Modern tweens communicate through constant, low-level connections, which raise expectations about availability and response times. Text messaging, social media comments, and gaming chat provide continuous social contact, making traditional "catching up" conversations feel unnecessary or artificial.

This constant connection offers benefits, including immediate support during difficult moments, sustained relationships despite distance or scheduling conflicts, and opportunities for shy children to develop social confidence through digital interaction before translating those skills into face-to-face situations.

However, continuous communication also creates pressure for immediate responses, anxiety about being left out of ongoing conversations, and difficulty developing comfort with solitude or independent thought processing. The notification culture means that social interaction competes with every other activity for attention and focus.

ENTERTAINMENT AND MEDIA: From Appointment Television to Algorithm Curation

The shift from scheduled, shared entertainment experiences to personalized, on-demand content has transformed how tweens relate to media, develop cultural knowledge, and share experiences with peers and family. In 1990, entertainment operated on an appointment basis. Saturday-morning cartoons, prime-time family shows, and movie-theater releases created shared cultural experiences in which entire generations watched the same content at the same time. Children developed patience for delayed gratification – waiting for their show's time slot, anticipating movie release dates, and accepting that missed episodes might be gone forever.

This shared viewing created common cultural references that facilitated social bonding. Children could assume their peers had seen the same shows, heard the same songs, and experienced the same entertainment milestones, creating natural conversation starters and shared understanding.

When I mentioned that if you missed an episode of your favorite show, it was just gone – likely forever – Bash asked why you wouldn't just watch it on the app. I explained there were no apps. No streaming. No DVR. If you missed it, you missed it, unless it showed up in summer reruns months later. He processed this information like I'd described a natural disaster. 'That's so sad,' he said.

Family entertainment often required negotiation and compromise. With limited television channels and one family television, everyone had to agree on programming or take turns choosing shows. This meant exposure to a wider range of genres and whatever was deemed "age-appropriate," while also building serious family compromise skills. I told my kids the other day, "When I was your age, we had like 10 channels, and we were happy with them." The second it left my mouth, I realized I've become my father. (sigh)

Modern tweens access virtually unlimited entertainment through streaming services, video platforms, and gaming libraries, with content tailored to their individual preferences. Algorithm curation means they primarily encounter content similar to what they've already enjoyed, creating more refined but potentially narrower entertainment experiences.

Personalization offers significant advantages, including exposure to diverse content that matches their interests, the ability to explore topics in depth, and freedom from inappropriate content that might appear during shared family viewing. Children with niche interests can find communities and content that help them feel less alone in their passions.

However, algorithm-driven entertainment also creates filter bubbles that limit exposure to diverse perspectives, reduce tolerance for content that doesn't immediately engage them, and eliminate many opportunities to develop compromise skills around shared entertainment choices. The effort required to choose from unlimited options can exceed the energy available for enjoying selected content.

I've watched Mara spend forty-five minutes scrolling through Netflix trying to find something to watch, only to give up and go back to a show she's already seen three times. When I pointed out that she'd spent longer choosing than she would have spent watching, she said, 'Yeah, but what if I picked wrong?' I replied, 'Back in my day, we watched whatever was on, and we were grateful.' The phrase 'back in my day' should come with a warning label. Once you say it, you can't unsay it. You're officially old now.

Academic and Career Preparation: From Industrial to Information Age

What it means to 'be prepared for the future' has completely changed – and that shift creates serious generation-gap confusion between parents and kids. Back in 1990, schools focused on specific skills built around assumptions about adult work that have aged about as well as dial-up internet. Memorization, handwriting, research that required actual *library stamina*, and comfort with linear, step-by-step learning prepared students for careers that rewarded information retention and procedural execution. Basically, "know the thing, do the thing, repeat the thing, and try not to lose your floppy disk."

Many careers offered clear advancement paths where employees could expect to stay with a single company for decades, build expertise in specific areas, and advance through predictable hierarchies. Educational preparation focused on foundational skills that would serve students throughout careers in relatively stable fields.

Bash asked me what he should be when he grows up. I started to answer, then realized that half the jobs that will exist when he's an adult probably don't exist yet. When I was his age, 'social media manager' and 'app developer' weren't careers because social media and apps weren't things. His future job may not yet have a name. That's either exciting or terrifying, depending on how much coffee I've had. What predicts success now includes digital literacy, cross-border and cross-cultural collaboration, comfort with ambiguity, and the ability to learn new systems quickly.

This shift creates challenges for parents who have relied on familiar strategies and may struggle to understand why their proven approaches don't have the same impact on their children. The advice that helped previous generations – study hard, follow rules, respect authority, stay with good companies – can miss the mark for kids growing up in a more fluid, uncertain career landscape. Tweens today need to build healthier relationships with failure, uncertainty, and change. Where earlier generations could master a skill once and rely on it for years, modern kids need comfort with constant adaptation and ongoing learning. Basically, life is a series of updates… and they didn't even get to click "remind me later."

Independence and Safety: From Free-Range to Structured Supervision

No area illustrates generational differences more clearly than childhood independence and safety management. The shift from primarily external threats to increased awareness of various dangers has changed how children experience autonomy and risk-taking.

In 1990, children typically had significantly more unsupervised time and greater freedom to explore their environments independently. Walking or biking to school, playing outside until dark without specific destinations or supervision, and managing personal schedules with minimal adult involvement were typical childhood experiences that built confidence, resourcefulness, and self-reliance.

The limited communication technology meant that children learned to handle unexpected situations independently rather than immediately calling for adult assistance. Getting lost, dealing with minor injuries, or navigating social conflicts without immediate parental intervention taught resilience and resourcefulness.

This independence came with real risks that modern parents often find unacceptable. Children faced genuine dangers from traffic, strangers, and unsupervised activities, but these risks were generally accepted as standard parts of childhood, seen as building character and competence.

Modern childhood involves significantly more structured supervision and safety management. Increased awareness of various threats, legal liability concerns, and technological capabilities for constant communication have altered expectations about adult oversight and child independence.

I catch myself doing this from time to time. Bash wanted to bike to his friend's house up the street, and my first instinct was to drive him. Not because it's dangerous – I biked farther than that alone when I was his age – but because the mental calculus has shifted. What if something happens? What if he needs me? Sim has to remind me that letting him go is part of raising him. It's still hard to watch him pedal away.

Today's tweens often have fewer opportunities to practice independent decision-making, solve problems without adult consultation, or manage minor risks and failures without immediate intervention. While this protection prevents many potential harms, it also limits opportunities to develop confidence and competence through independent experience.

The challenge for modern parents involves finding an appropriate balance between necessary protection and independence-building experiences. Creating safe opportunities for controlled risk-taking and independent decision-making requires intentional effort rather than natural environmental conditions.

Building Bridges Across Generational Understanding

Rather than viewing these changes as proof that the past or present "did it better," parents benefit from understanding how shifting environmental factors shaped each generation's experience – and continue shaping their children's development.

Your childhood, shaped by a different technological and social era, developed skills and perspectives that served you well but may not translate directly to your child's world. Your ability to memorize phone numbers and go 12 hours without a charger is both impressive and deeply confusing to them. Likewise, your child's adaptations to today's environment are building skills and perspectives that will serve them in the future, even if they don't look like what worked for you – because their world comes with push notifications, algorithmic peer pressure, and homework that somehow requires three apps and a password reset.

Recognizing these differences helps you respond with empathy instead of frustration. When they struggle with patience, prefer digital communication, or seem overwhelmed by choices, they're demonstrating normal adaptation to their environment rather than deficient character development.

Understanding generational differences also helps identify valuable skills and experiences from your background that can benefit your child despite technological changes. Teaching them to enjoy delayed gratification, develop face-to-face interaction, and appreciate non-digital experiences provides balance without rejecting their digital native capabilities.

Creating family traditions that blend generational strengths helps children appreciate a range of approaches while keeping a connection to family history and values. Sharing stories about your childhood experiences, teaching them skills from your generation, and learning about their world creates mutual respect and understanding.

The goal isn't to recreate your childhood for them or to fully embrace every aspect of modern childhood, but to help them develop skills and perspectives that serve them well in the world they're actually living in—while still staying grounded in meaningful traditions and relationships that bridge generations.

Appreciating Both Then and Now

Understanding the dramatic changes between 1990 and 2025 tweenhood doesn't mean judging either era as superior or inferior. Both generations faced unique challenges and opportunities that shaped different strengths and perspectives.

Your childhood equipped you with skills and experiences that serve you well as an adult, while your child's current experiences are preparing them for their future adult responsibilities. The key lies in recognizing both sets of strengths while helping your child navigate their real world rather than the one you remember.

The young person living in your home is navigating a world that would have seemed like science fiction when you were their age. Their challenges are real and significant, even when they look nothing like the challenges you faced. Sometimes I watch Mara or Bash struggle with something I never had to deal with – algorithmic social pressure, infinite content choices, friendships that exist entirely through screens – and I have to remind myself that 'different' doesn't mean 'easier.' Their hard is just a different kind of hard.

eight
how to (actually) talk to your tween

Communicating with your tween can sometimes feel like mediating a high-stakes standoff in a language you're still learning; you're experiencing the normal challenge of bridging generational perspectives while respecting their developing independence. The stakes feel high because these conversations shape your relationship for years to come, but the rules keep changing as they grow and their needs evolve.

Talking to a tween is nothing like talking to a little kid, and it's definitely not like talking to another adult. It's its own strange art form – part negotiation, part mind-reading, part knowing when to shut up. You're engaging with someone who possesses adult-level thinking capacity in some areas while still developing emotional regulation and social awareness in others. They want to be treated with respect and autonomy while still needing guidance and support – creating a dance that requires constant adjustment, and occasionally stepping on each other's toes.

The Art of Reading Between the Lines

Learning to interpret tween communication means recognizing that what they say doesn't always match what they mean – not because they're being deliberately deceptive, but because they're still developing the vocabulary and confidence to express big, tangled feelings directly. The phrase "I'm fine" is one of the most suspicious words in the English language when spoken by a tween with crossed arms. This response can mean anything from genuine contentment to overwhelming emotional distress, and distinguishing between them requires attention to context, body language, and recent patterns rather than accepting the words at face value.

When "I'm fine" arrives with crossed arms, averted eye contact, and a tone that could freeze water, they're usually saying something is definitely wrong, but they're not ready to discuss it yet. This might reflect processing time needs, uncertainty about how to articulate their feelings, or a test of whether you'll pursue the conversation despite their initial deflection.

Last week I asked Mara how school was. 'Fine,' she said, in a tone that suggested school had personally wronged her and she was considering legal action. I asked if something had happened. 'No.' Was she sure? 'Yes.' Did she want to talk about anything? Heavy sigh. 'Mom, I said I'm fine.' She was not fine. I made her favorite snack and waited. Twenty minutes later, the whole story came out. Sometimes 'fine' is a timer, not an answer.

Sometimes "I'm fine" actually means they're managing their situation on their own and genuinely don't need parental intervention. Learning to distinguish between these scenarios prevents both unnecessary worry and missed opportunities to provide needed support.

The silent treatment often communicates more effectively than words, though interpreting the message requires careful observation. Sudden quietness may indicate disappointment with the processing, a sense of being misunderstood, or a withdrawal to avoid saying something they'll regret. It can also signal that they're wrestling with problems they don't feel ready to share, or that they hope you'll notice their distress without asking for help directly.

Rather than immediately demanding explanations for silent behavior, try offering gentle availability: "I notice you seem quiet today. I'm here if you want to talk, and it's okay if you don't." Translation: 'I see you're upset, and I'm not going anywhere, but I'm also not going to force you to talk.' It's the parenting equivalent of leaving the door open.

Explosive reactions to minor issues frequently indicate accumulated stress rather than genuine distress about the immediate trigger. When they melt down over a homework assignment, misplaced item, or minor schedule change, they might be releasing pressure from multiple sources that have been building without obvious outlets.

Understanding this pattern helps you address the underlying stress rather than just the surface complaint. Instead of focusing on why homework shouldn't cause tears, you might acknowledge that they seem overwhelmed and ask about other pressures they're managing.

Timing and Environment: When and Where Conversations Happen

Successful tween discussions often depend more on timing and setting than on perfect word choices or brilliant insights. Understanding when they're most receptive and where they feel comfortable lays the foundation for meaningful connection.

Car conversations offer unique advantages for discussing sensitive topics: the shared activity reduces pressure from direct eye contact, and the natural boundaries of travel time provide a sense of safety. Many tweens find it easier to discuss personal issues when they're not facing interrogation-style questioning across a table. The confined space also prevents either party from walking away during difficult discussions, while the shared focus on travel destinations provides natural topic transitions when conversations become too intense. Some of the most important family discussions happen during routine drives rather than formal sit-down meetings.

Some of my best conversations with Bash happen in the car on the way to soccer practice. There's something about both of us facing forward, no eye contact required, that makes him willing to talk about things he'd never bring up at the dinner table. Last month, he told me about a kid who was being mean to his friend – a conversation that never would have happened if I'd sat him down and asked directly. Now I actually enjoy carting the kids around.

Bedtime conversations can create intimate opportunities for sharing as the day's activities wind down and defenses naturally lower. The darkness often makes personal disclosure feel safer, while the transition toward sleep encourages honest reflection rather than performance-based interaction.

However, bedtime timing also requires sensitivity to their energy levels and processing needs. Overwhelming them with serious discussions when they're tired can backfire, while gentle check-ins about daily experiences often yield surprising insights into their inner lives.

Activity-based conversations work well for tweens who struggle with direct verbal dialogue. Working together on projects, cooking, walking, or sharing hobbies creates natural opportunities for discussion while reducing the pressure of formal conversation.

The shared focus on external activities often allows personal topics to emerge organically rather than feeling forced or artificial. Many parent-child relationships deepen through consistent shared activities that create regular opportunities for natural connection.

Kitchen counter conversations during snack preparation or homework time often provide ideal circumstances for casual check-ins that can evolve into deeper discussions. The informal setting and routine activity create a relaxed environment where important topics can emerge without feeling like planned interventions. Never attempt a serious conversation when they're hungry. Actually, never attempt anything when they're hungry. Feed them first, talk second. This applies to adults, too, honestly.

The Power of Brave Questions

Traditional parenting questions like "How was school?" or "What did you do today?" rarely produce meaningful responses because they're too broad and feel like routine inquiries rather than a genuine interest in their experience. Brave questions demonstrate specific curiosity about their world while creating opportunities for authentic sharing.

Instead of asking about their entire day, try focusing on specific aspects that show you've been paying attention to their interests and concerns. Questions like "How did that math test go that you were worried about?" or "Did you get to sit with Gabi at lunch like you hoped?" demonstrate that you remember details from previous conversations and care about outcomes.

Questions about emotions work better when they're specific rather than general.

INSTEAD OF "How was school?" TRY:

- "What made you laugh today?"
- "Was there any moment today when you felt proud of yourself?"
- "Who did you sit with at lunch?"
- "Did anything surprise you today?"
- "What's one thing you learned that you didn't know yesterday?"
- "If you could change one thing about today, what would it be?"

FOR DEEPER CONVERSATIONS:

- "What's something you wish I understood better about your life right now?"
- "Is there anything you've been wanting to talk about but haven't found the right time?"

- "What's something your friends are dealing with that seems hard?"
- "If you could make one rule for our family, what would it be?"
- "What's something I do that embarrasses you?" (Warning: this will generate a longer list than you're prepared for. Ask at your own risk.)

These approaches invite positive sharing while creating opportunities to discuss challenges if they choose to elaborate.

Hypothetical questions can help tweens explore values and decision-making without feeling personally judged. Asking "What would you do if you saw someone being excluded at lunch?" or "How do you think someone should handle it when friends disagree?" allows them to share their thinking about situations they might face without admitting to current struggles.

Questions about their friends and social situations often yield more information than direct inquiries about their own experiences. Tweens frequently feel more comfortable discussing what's happening with others before sharing their own challenges, and these conversations often reveal their values and concerns indirectly.

The key to brave questions is genuine curiosity, not hidden agendas. When your questions serve your need for information or control rather than their need for connection and understanding, they quickly recognize the difference and respond accordingly.

Navigating the Step-In vs. Step-Back Decision

The most challenging aspect of talking with your tween is knowing when situations call for parental intervention and when they need space to develop independence and problem-solving skills. This balance shifts constantly as they mature and their circumstances change.

Safety always warrants stepping in – but in the tween years, 'safety' means more than physical harm. Emotional safety, social safety, and psychological well-being matter just as much, even if protecting them looks different.

When bullying, cyberbullying, or social cruelty affects your tween, stepping in becomes necessary even when they prefer to handle situations independently. However, the manner of intervention requires careful consideration of their developmental needs and social dynamics. I once intervened in a friendship conflict Mara was having, thinking I was being helpful. I was not being helpful. She was mortified; the situation became more complicated, and she didn't tell me about the friend drama for months afterward. Lesson learned: unless someone's safety is at risk, my job is usually to listen and ask questions, not to fix. Sim has had to physically stop me from sending emails to other parents. He's usually right. Get yourself a Sim.

Academic struggles fall into gray areas where the step-in decision depends on multiple factors, including their effort level, available resources, and impact on self-esteem versus learning opportunities. Sometimes stepping back allows them to experience natural consequences that motivate future effort, while at other times intervention prevents problems from spiraling beyond their current capacity to manage.

Friendship drama typically benefits from a step-back approach unless patterns indicate unhealthy relationships or situations beyond typical social learning. Allowing them to navigate peer conflicts independently builds essential life skills, while premature parental involvement can create additional social complications.

The decision often involves assessing whether they possess the skills and resources needed to handle their situation successfully. When they lack the necessary tools or knowledge, providing guidance and support makes sense. When they have the capability but need practice, stepping back allows skill development.

Tell them why you're stepping in or stepping back. 'I'm not getting involved because I think you can handle this' means something different than just disappearing. 'I'm getting involved because this is a safety issue' is better than swooping in without explanation. Explaining why you're choosing to intervene or step back shows respect for their growing autonomy while still honoring your role as the parent.

Building Trust Through Consistent Responses

Trust between parents and tweens grows from predictable, reliable responses to their communication, rather than from perfect advice or instant problem-solving. They need to know that sharing difficult information won't result in dramatic overreactions, immediate punishments, or loss of privacy privileges.

When they share concerning information about themselves or their friends, your initial response determines whether they'll continue bringing problems to your attention. Responding with curiosity and support before moving to problem-solving builds their confidence in your ability to handle difficult information appropriately.

When Mara first told me about a classmate who was posting mean things about another kid online, I went into full panic mode – even though she wasn't involved. I started asking a hundred questions, suggesting we call the school, and wondering if I should contact the other parents. She immediately regretted telling me. Now I've learned to take a breath before responding. My first reaction determines whether she'll bring me the next piece of concerning news or keep it to herself. When minor mistakes lead to major parental meltdowns, they learn that honesty creates more problems than secrecy.

Consistency in your responses helps them predict your reactions and plan how they open up accordingly. When your response to similar situations varies dramatically with your mood, stress level, or external circumstances, they become reluctant to share because they can't gauge the potential consequences.

Respecting privacy builds trust while maintaining appropriate boundaries. They need to know that conversations with you won't automatically become family gossip, social media content, or stories shared with other parents unless safety issues require broader intervention.

Following through on commitments and agreements demonstrates reliability that encourages continued sharing. When you promise to consider requests, discuss issues with partners, or research solutions, actually doing so builds credibility for future conversations.

When Words Aren't Enough

Sometimes, when tweens communicate, parents must move beyond words to address underlying needs or provide support that words alone can't. Recognizing these situations prevents ongoing frustration with conversation-based approaches that don't align with their current needs.

Sometimes Bash doesn't want to talk about what's wrong — he just wants to sit next to me while I fold laundry or watch him play a video game. No questions, no advice, just presence. It took me a while to understand that sitting quietly together IS the conversation sometimes. Some tweens process feelings through movement, creative expression, or quiet companionship rather than talking.

Practical support often communicates love more clearly than verbal reassurance during stressful periods. Helping with homework, providing favorite snacks, managing logistical challenges, or simply reducing their daily stress load demonstrates care through action rather than words.

Sometimes outside support becomes necessary – when your conversations aren't getting through, or when the problem is bigger than your family can handle alone. Recognizing when situations require therapeutic intervention protects both your relationship and their well-being.

Sometimes stepping away from the situation allows natural resolution of temporary conflicts or emotional storms. Tweens often need processing time between conversations, and pushing for an immediate resolution can prolong, rather than resolve, difficulties.

Creative approaches work well for tweens who struggle with direct verbal sharing. Written notes, shared journals, artistic expression, or digital communication can provide alternative channels for connection when face-to-face conversation feels too challenging.

Growing Into Deeper Connection

The communication patterns you develop during your child's tween years will influence your relationship throughout their adolescence and into adulthood. Investing in patient, respectful dialogue now lays the foundation for continued connection as people move through increasingly independent life stages.

As they develop a stronger identity and values, conversations become more sophisticated and rewarding. The tween who struggles to articulate feelings today may become the young adult who seeks your perspective on major life decisions tomorrow. I got a glimpse of this recently. Mara, unprompted, asked me what I was like at her age. Not in a 'leave me alone' way – in a genuinely curious way. We talked for twenty minutes about my tween years, my friendships, and my embarrassing moments. It wasn't a breakthrough. It was just... a conversation. The kind I've been working toward. The kind that makes all the difficult ones worth it.

Knowing that meaningful conversations don't happen overnight helps maintain realistic expectations during difficult periods. The capacity for deep, meaningful conversation emerges over time through consistent practice rather than suddenly appearing when they reach certain developmental milestones.

You're modeling what healthy relationships look like, and they're taking notes – even when it seems like they're not paying attention. When you demonstrate active listening, emotional regulation, conflict resolution, and respectful disagreement, you're providing templates for their future interactions.

When they actually talk to you – really talk – don't let the moment pass without acknowledging it. That's how you get more moments like it. When conversations go well, recognizing the positive interaction reinforces their willingness to engage openly in future discussions.

The Long Game of Connection

Reaching your tween requires patience, flexibility, and faith in the long-term relationship you're building together. The child who shuts you out today is slowly developing the skills to let you in – and that will pay off in the adult relationship you'll have tomorrow.

Every conversation attempt, whether successful or unsuccessful, reinforces their understanding that you're available for dialogue and interested in their perspective. This foundation of availability and respect creates a sense of security that encourages them to continue bringing their questions, concerns, and experiences to your attention.

The goal isn't perfect communication or immediate understanding, but a relatively consistent demonstration that you value connection with them and respect their developing autonomy. These principles guide your interactions through inevitable challenges while building toward deeper mutual understanding.

Your tween is learning to navigate complex emotions and expanding their social world while staying connected to family members who knew them as children—and are still adjusting to who they're becoming. Your patience with this process demonstrates that relationships can evolve and deepen rather than simply grow more distant as people change.

nine
health, hygiene, and survival hacks

Maintaining basic human cleanliness and wellness with your tween can feel like negotiating peace treaties with a tiny dictator who's convinced soap is optional and vegetables are war crimes. Congratulations—you've officially entered the hygiene resistance phase of parenting. This is the season where your sweet child transforms into someone who views showering as cruel and unusual punishment, while mysteriously developing the ability to survive entirely on air-popped snacks and existential dread.

The beautiful irony of tween hygiene is that they care deeply about their appearance while simultaneously believing that deodorant is a conspiracy theory and shampoo is merely a suggestion. They'll spend forty-five minutes perfecting their hair only to refuse to wash it for a week, creating a fascinating study in contradictory priorities that would baffle behavioral scientists.

Bath Time or Lye Time?: The Great Shower Standoff

Remember when bath time was fun? When rubber ducks and bubble beards brought joy to the whole household? Those days are officially over. Welcome to the era where suggesting a shower earns you the same reaction you'd get from announcing an unexpected pop quiz – or a surprise family meeting.

Your tween now approaches water with the enthusiasm of a cat being introduced to a swimming pool. They've developed elaborate theories about why daily showers are "unnecessary" and "bad for the environment," conveniently ignoring the fact that their current aroma could be classified as its own ecosystem.

The shower negotiation process resembles haggling at a car dealership – except the salesperson is nine and has no concept of compromise. You'll find yourself making bargains just to close the deal: "If you shower today, you can pick tomorrow's dinner," or "Five minutes in there, and I'll consider extending your curfew by exactly three minutes next month."

They've somehow convinced themselves that standing near the bathroom while the shower runs counts as personal hygiene, creating elaborate alibis involving "steam cleaning" and "aromatherapy benefits." You'll discover evidence of their deception in the form of completely dry towels and suspiciously unchanged hair situations. Bash once emerged from the bathroom after 'showering' with completely dry hair. When I pointed this out, he said, 'I washed the important parts.' I asked him to define 'important parts.' He could not. Back to the bathroom, he went.

The physics of tween showering defies all known laws of nature. They can enter a bathroom with enough hot water to supply a small village and emerge fifteen minutes later, claiming they "ran out of time". Yet, the bathroom looks like a hurricane hit it, but they somehow remain unchanged by the experience.

When they finally shower, they approach soap as if it were radioactive, using approximately one molecule of shampoo and declaring themselves "clean enough for government work." They've mastered the art of getting wet without actually washing anything, which is quite an achievement when you think about it.

Getting them to enjoy showers means basically turning your bathroom into a spa – waterproof speakers (or allow them to put their iPad on the toilet seat), perfect water pressure, and towels that meet their exacting standards. You're creating a resort experience for someone who thinks soap is optional. You might find yourself installing waterproof speakers, adjusting water pressure to their exact specifications, or providing specialized towels that meet their increasingly demanding comfort requirements. You're creating a spa experience for someone who believes hygiene is optional.

Deodorant: The Mysterious Stick of Adult Responsibility

We covered the initial deodorant introduction in Chapter 2 – the first conversation, the confusion, and the selection process. This section covers what happens next: introducing deodorant is one thing; getting them to actually use it every day is another thing entirely.

The problem isn't that they don't understand deodorant. They get it. They just don't remember it exists until approximately three seconds after leaving the house, at which point it's somehow your fault that they smell like a gym locker. Bash has walked past his deodorant, which sits directly next to his toothbrush, every morning for six months. He sees it. He just doesn't register it as something that applies to him on this particular day.

You'll become the household smell detector, developing a sixth sense for skipped applications. I can identify a deodorant-free child from across the room, usually during car rides where escape is impossible. The question "Bash, Did you put on deodorant this morning?" will come out of your mouth so often that it loses meaning, like a word you've repeated too many times.

The excuses become creative. "I put some on yesterday." "I didn't sweat today." "I'm pretty sure I did?" My personal favorite from Bash: "I was going to, but then I forgot, and then I remembered, but by then I was already downstairs, so." The logic is airtight if you don't think about it.

Strategic placement helps. We now have deodorant in the bathroom, the bedroom, the car, and my purse. Backup deodorant is not paranoia – it's survival planning. Mara has learned to keep one in her locker after a regrettable incident in PE class that she's asked me never to discuss in detail.

The goal is making it automatic, like brushing teeth – something they do without thinking because it's just part of the routine. We're not there yet. Some days I wonder if we'll ever get there. But every morning that they remember without prompting feels like a small victory, a sign that eventually, perhaps, this will become their responsibility instead of mine.

Until then, I sniff. I remind. I strategically place backup supplies. And I remind myself that someday they'll be adults who manage their own hygiene without parental oversight – even if that day feels very, very far away.

Acne Adventures: When Faces Rebel

The arrival of acne represents your tween's first real betrayal by their own body, and they handle this development with all the emotional regulation of a soap opera character facing their first heartbreak.

One day, they have baby-smooth skin that makes moisturizer commercials jealous; the next day, they wake up looking like an aggressive connect-the-dots puzzle has attacked them. The overnight transformation leaves them staring in mirrors with the horror – the same stare they give when they discover the Wi-Fi password has been changed.

Their initial response to acne usually involves either completely ignoring it (hoping it will magically disappear through willpower alone) or attacking it with the intensity of someone performing emergency surgery with kitchen utensils. There's rarely middle ground between denial and full-scale warfare. Mara once asked me if people at school could 'see' a pimple that was so small I needed her to point directly at it before I could find it. To her, it was a billboard. To everyone else, it was invisible. I've learned that 'I don't even notice it' is not reassuring – what she needs to hear is 'I see it, and it's not a big deal, and it will be gone in a few days.' Acknowledging the pimple's existence while minimizing its importance is the balance she needs.

When they choose an attack method, they'll use every available product, often simultaneously, creating chemical combinations that would make chemists nervous. Their bathroom counter becomes a laboratory where expensive face washes mix with home remedies sourced from questionable online sources. The mirror becomes their greatest enemy and closest confidant. They'll spend extended periods examining every pore with microscopic intensity, convinced that everyone they encounter will immediately focus on the minor blemish they've decided represents social catastrophe. They develop elaborate theories about the causes of acne that rarely draw on medical evidence. Pizza becomes the enemy, chocolate gets blamed for everything, and homework-related stress is identified as the primary culprit, conveniently ignoring that they're experiencing a completely normal biological process.

Getting expert help becomes necessary when their bedroom starts resembling a dermatology clinic, and they begin avoiding social situations because of skin concerns. Finding the right dermatologist becomes another parenting adventure, as they need someone who can communicate with teenagers without triggering defensive responses.

The emotional support required during acne adventures often exceeds the medical intervention. You'll find yourself providing daily reassurance that temporary skin issues don't determine permanent social status, while secretly hoping their confidence recovers faster than their complexion.

Feeding the Bottomless Pit: Nutrition in the Cheeto Era

Growth spurts transform your previously reasonable eater into what appears to be a human garbage disposal with opinions.

They can consume their own body weight in snacks and still claim to be starving five minutes later, creating grocery bills that rival small-country budgets.

Their appetite timing seems designed to maximize parental inconvenience. They'll declare complete food disinterest during mealtimes, then experience urgent hunger exactly when all stores are closed and only expired crackers remain in the pantry. The bottomless pit phenomenon means they can empty your refrigerator faster than a power outage, leaving behind only condiments and that mysterious container of leftovers nobody wants to investigate. You'll find yourself shopping for groceries every other day while wondering if you're accidentally feeding additional families.

Their taste preferences become increasingly ridiculous and contradictory. They'll request "exactly like McDonald's but healthier" or "pizza but with vegetables that don't taste like vegetables." Meeting these specifications requires a lot more creativity. Vegetables become the enemy in ways that would make medieval warfare look peaceful. They can detect microscopic amounts of green substances hidden in any dish and will conduct thorough investigations to ensure no nutritious content has infiltrated their preferred carbohydrate consumption. The snack negotiation process resembles a courtroom plea deal – lots of bargaining, very little mercy. You'll find yourself bargaining over fruit before cookie access and inventing elaborate veggie point systems that would make an accountant reach for a spreadsheet.

They develop selective amnesia about previous food preferences. Things they loved last week become "disgusting" without warning, while foods they've never expressed interest in suddenly become "the only thing they can eat." Menu planning becomes an exercise in predicting rapidly changing preferences.

Cooking for growth spurts requires the kind of strategic planning you'd expect from a logistics team. You'll learn to double every recipe, hide vegetables in increasingly creative ways, and maintain emergency snack reserves that could sustain a small expedition. Bash can eat an entire box of cereal in one sitting and then, forty-five minutes later, ask what's for dinner, as if the cereal never happened. I've started buying groceries like I'm preparing for a natural disaster. Sim says I'm overreacting, but he isn't there for the 'snack break' after school.

Sleep Wars: The Midnight Rebellion

Your tween's relationship with sleep is a complicated romantic drama where u at? both parties clash over what they want, and nobody's entirely sure how to fix it. They need more sleep than ever before, but resist bedtime with the determination of freedom fighters. Their natural sleep cycle shifts toward staying up later and sleeping later, which unfortunately doesn't align with school schedules designed by people who clearly never experienced teenage biology. You're caught between honoring their biological needs and meeting society's expectations about morning functionality.

Bedtime becomes a negotiation that starts around dinner and continues until you're too tired to maintain your position. They'll present compelling arguments about homework requirements, social obligations, and the critical importance of completing just one more level of whatever they're playing. Mara claims she 'can't fall asleep' before midnight but somehow passes out instantly during any family movie. Last week, she slept through an entire action sequence with explosions, then was wide awake at 11:30 PM, 'not tired at all.' The science doesn't make sense, but here we are.

The bedroom transforms into an entertainment hub, equipped with more electronic devices than most offices. Their bed becomes a command center where they can simultaneously text friends, watch videos, do homework, and technically "rest" without actually sleeping.

Screen time before bed affects their sleep quality, but removing devices can provoke reactions that make you think you've just announced a household-wide emergency. You'll find yourself in philosophical debates about blue light exposure with someone who considers your concern about melatonin production to be evidence of technological ignorance.

Morning wake-up routines require increasingly creative approaches as their sleep debt accumulates. You'll progress from gentle encouragement to air horn consideration, while they develop superhuman abilities to sleep through alarm systems that could wake neighboring counties.

They'll claim they "can't fall asleep" at reasonable bedtimes, yet somehow lose consciousness instantly during any daytime activity requiring attention. Their ability to fall asleep during family movies while remaining wide awake at midnight defies all logic.

Creating sleep-friendly environments is an interior design challenge that involves blackout curtains, white noise machines, temperature controls, and comfort requirements that would make luxury hotels envious. You're creating a sleep laboratory for someone who considers rest optional.

Building Habits Without Losing Your Mind

The transition from parent-managed to self-managed health routines requires more patience than it took to house-train our dog, Dawson, and more creativity than it takes to decorate wedding cakes. You're teaching someone to take responsibility for their body while they're still figuring out how their body works.

Habit formation with tweens follows the same principles as training cats – possible but requiring extraordinary patience and realistic expectations about compliance rates. What worked perfectly yesterday might be rejected entirely today for reasons that make sense only to them. Creating positive associations with health routines means making boring activities feel special without spending your entire budget on bathroom accessories. You'll find yourself celebrating the completion of a shower as you would academic achievements and treating deodorant application as a major life milestone.

The key to success involves making health requirements feel like personal choices rather than parental impositions. This takes presentation skills that could impress a seasoned marketer and negotiation chops strong enough to broker peace between siblings. Flexibility is essential when schedules change overnight, and preferences shift like sand dunes. Rigid health routines work great in theory, but fall apart in practice when you're dealing with humans who are still figuring out who they are.

Building intrinsic motivation requires connecting abstract concepts such as "health" to concrete outcomes they care about, such as social confidence or athletic performance. You'll become an expert at translating parental concerns into benefits relevant to tweens. Progress celebrations should focus on effort and consistency rather than perfection, because perfectionism kills motivation faster than criticism. Small improvements deserve recognition proportional to major achievements in their developmental context.

Survival of the Freshest

You've now survived the crash course in tween health and hygiene management, from shower battles to deodorant introduction ceremonies and sleep schedule interventions that test your commitment to family harmony.

Remember that resistance to health routines often represents a struggle with independence rather than personal failure on anyone's part. They're learning to manage bodies that are changing faster than they can keep up with, while you're trying to guide someone who's simultaneously rejecting and needing your help.

The habits they develop during these years will influence their adult self-care, but the process doesn't have to be perfect to be effective. Consistency matters more than compliance, and relationship preservation often trumps immediate hygiene victories. Your patience during these daily negotiations teaches them that health routines can be manageable rather than overwhelming. At the same time, your sense of humor about the process helps everyone maintain perspective about what's truly important.

Keep your expectations realistic, your sense of humor intact, and a bottle of wine on standby should you need it. You're not just enforcing family hygiene standards—you're teaching someone how to take care of themselves for the rest of their life, one deodorant application and shower negotiation at a time.

ten
survive & (mostly) thrive: parenting strategies

This is your victory lap (with strategic pit stops for sanity maintenance). You've earned your unofficial degree in tween management - from decoding mysterious acronyms that change faster than fashion trends to riding out mood swings that can knock anyone off balance. If you've made it this far without requiring emergency chocolate intervention or developing stress-induced superpowers, you deserve recognition on the level of an Olympic medal ceremony.

But surviving tweendom isn't just about making it through each day with your sanity marginally intact - it's about building strategies that help your family not just endure this phase but actually discover moments of joy, connection, and genuine laughter amid the beautiful chaos. Think of this chapter as your advanced tactical manual for days when "good enough" parenting feels like heroic accomplishment.

Humor as Life Support: When Laughter Becomes Medicine

If you've learned anything from this adventure, it's that humor isn't just the cherry on top of your parenting sundae - it's the entire foundation that prevents the whole structure from collapsing into a puddle of tears and regret. When the going gets tough, the tough develop comedy routines about their daily survival experiences.

Tweendom provides endless material for a family comedy show, from voice cracks that could shatter glass to outfit choices that look as if they were assembled in the dark during a power outage. The key is learning to laugh with your tween rather than at them, creating shared humor that builds connection rather than embarrassment that drives them into permanent hiding.

Stress-busting through laughter is more effective than any prescription medication, though combining both approaches never hurts. When you feel your blood pressure rising because there's somehow a third sock floating in the toilet (again), pause, take a breath, and find the absurdity in the situation before addressing the practical problem of sock-fishing and bathroom hygiene lectures.

The timing of humor demands skillful tact – one wrong joke and the whole treaty collapses. Cracking jokes during active meltdowns rarely improves the situation, but finding comedic moments during calmer periods helps everyone maintain perspective on the temporary nature of tween drama and the universal absurdity of family life.

Document the chaos discreetly, because someday you'll want evidence that this phase actually happened and wasn't just an extended fever dream. Keep a private collection of quotes, photos, and incidents that showcase the unintentional comedy of tween life, but resist the urge to share these immediately on social media, where they might become permanent sources of embarrassment.

Creating family comedy traditions helps everyone appreciate the lighter side of daily challenges while building shared memories that strengthen relationships. Possibly it's weekly "quote of the week" nominations, where everyone contributes funny things they've heard, or monthly "epic fail" celebrations where family members share their most spectacular mistakes without judgment.

Family Meetings: Not for Everyone, But Maybe for You

Our first family meeting was a disaster. Bash spent the entire time making fart noises. Mara declared the concept "cringe" and asked to be excused. Sim and I sat there wondering why we thought this would work. But we tried the next week, with snacks. And the week after that. Now, three months in, they actually bring up topics they want to discuss. Bash still makes occasional fart noises, but progress is progress.

Family meetings aren't for everyone. Some families thrive with structured weekly check-ins; others find them forced and awkward, no matter how many times they try. If the concept makes everyone in your house groan, skip it – there are other ways to communicate. But if you're curious, here's what worked for us: neutral timing (Sunday after dinner, when everyone's fed and relatively calm), ground rules that feel fair (everyone speaks, no interruptions, complaints must include suggested solutions), and always ending with something good (choosing next week's movie, planning a fun outing, or just dessert).

The secret ingredient, honestly, was lowering our expectations. We stopped trying to resolve major family conflicts and started using meetings for practical logistics – who needs to be where this week, what's coming up, does anyone have concerns they want to raise? The big stuff still happens in car rides and kitchen counter conversations. But having a regular time when everyone sits down together, even imperfectly, has made those spontaneous conversations easier as well.

Professional Backup: A Quick Reminder

We covered warning signs and when to seek professional help in Chapter 4, so I won't repeat all of that here. As we wrap up, I want to reinforce something important: asking for help is not a failure. It's good parenting.

Whether it's a therapist for anxiety that isn't responding to your best efforts, a tutor for math that's become a nightly battlefield, or a specialist for attention issues that are affecting schoolwork, getting the right support means you're taking their needs seriously. Finding the right fit might take trial and error. The first therapist might not click. The tutor might need to be switched. That's normal, not a sign you made the wrong call.

The framing matters too. When Mara was diagnosed with ADHD, we didn't present it as something being wrong with her. We told her this explains why some things feel harder for you than for other kids – and now we can get you the right support. Her diagnosis wasn't a label; it was a roadmap. It helped her teachers understand what she needed, helped us adjust our expectations, and most importantly, helped her understand herself. She still has hard days, but now she has language for what's happening and tools that actually work for her brain. Getting that diagnosis was one of the best parenting decisions we've made.

Building Resilience: Yours and Theirs

Resilience isn't about preventing difficulties or having constant emotional equilibrium – it's about developing the ability to recover from setbacks, learn from challenges, and sustain hope during difficult periods. Both you and your tween need these skills, though building them requires patience and practice.

Resilience isn't about protecting them from failure – it's about showing them that failure won't destroy them. When Mara bombed a test she'd studied for, my instinct was to call the teacher, question the grading, and find someone to blame. Instead, I sat with her disappointment, told her it happens to everyone, and watched her figure out what to do differently next time. Hardest parenting moment of the month. Also, maybe the most important. When they experience disappointment, resist the urge to solve their problems immediately or explain why the situation isn't really that bad. Instead, validate their feelings while expressing confidence in their ability to handle challenges.

Encourage problem-solving by asking questions that guide them toward solutions rather than providing answers immediately. Questions such as "What do you think might help in this situation?" or "What would you tell a friend dealing with this problem?" help them develop independent thinking while knowing you're available for support. Model resilience by sharing your own experiences with setbacks and recovery in age-appropriate ways that demonstrate perseverance without overwhelming them with adult concerns. When you make mistakes, show them how you handle disappointment, make repairs, and move forward without catastrophizing or giving up entirely.

Create opportunities for controlled risk-taking that allow them to experience manageable challenges and build confidence in handling uncertainty. This might involve trying new activities, taking on appropriate responsibilities, or making decisions with natural consequences that aren't too severe.

Building your own resilience requires recognizing that parenting tweens is inherently challenging and that struggling doesn't indicate personal failure or inadequate preparation. Set realistic expectations about daily functioning, celebrate small victories, and maintain connections with other adults who understand the unique challenges of this developmental stage.

Develop self-care practices that sustain you through difficult periods without requiring elaborate planning or significant time investments. This might involve brief daily activities that restore your energy, regular connection with supportive friends, or simple rituals that provide comfort during stressful times.

The Long Game: Perspective for the Marathon

Parenting tweens requires an endurance mindset rather than sprint energy, as this phase lasts several years and requires a sustainable pace. Keeping perspective about temporary challenges while building a foundation for long-term relationship success helps you make decisions that serve your family's ultimate goals.

Remember that your tween's current behavior reflects their developmental stage rather than their permanent personality or your parenting effectiveness. The child who seems impossible to reach today is developing the thinking and communication skills that will allow for a rich adult relationship tomorrow, even when daily evidence suggests otherwise.

Sometimes I have to ask myself: Is this battle worth winning if it damages our relationship? The answer is usually no. The homework will get done, or it won't. The room will get cleaned eventually. But if every interaction becomes a fight, I lose something more important than a tidy bedroom. Pick your battles. Lose some on purpose. The relationship is the long game. Sometimes choosing your battles means accepting imperfect outcomes to maintain trust and communication that support long-term family harmony.

Document positive moments and progress that might get overshadowed by daily challenges, because perspective requires evidence that good things are happening alongside the difficulties. Keep records of funny conversations, sweet interactions, and signs of growing maturity that remind you of your child's wonderful qualities during frustrating periods.

Invest in activities and traditions that create positive shared experiences, even when scheduling feels impossible, and cooperation seems unlikely. These investments in family connections build goodwill that sustains relationships through inevitable difficult periods.

Maintain realistic expectations about your family's functioning during this phase, recognizing that some areas may need to shift temporarily while you focus your energy on essential priorities. Perfect household management might be impossible while navigating emotional crises, and that's acceptable as long as everyone's basic needs are met.

Plan for gradual transitions toward independence rather than expecting sudden maturity, which rarely occurs on parental timelines. Your tween is learning to manage increasing responsibilities while still needing guidance and support, which requires patience for the back-and-forth nature of adolescent development.

Creating Your Family's Survival Toolkit

Every family needs customized strategies that reflect their unique personalities, circumstances, and challenges, because generic advice rarely addresses specific situations that arise in real-world family life. Building your toolkit involves collecting techniques that work for your particular combination of personalities and needs.

Identify your family's specific stress triggers and develop preventive strategies that reduce the likelihood of major conflicts during predictable difficult periods. It might be that mornings require extensive preparation the night before, or certain times of day need extra structure to prevent meltdowns.

Establish emergency protocols for urgent situations to ensure everyone knows what to expect when difficulties escalate beyond normal management. This might involve specific family members taking designated roles, predetermined consequences for certain behaviors, or automatic cooling-off procedures that prevent situations from spiraling.

Create comfort resources that provide emotional support during difficult periods, including physical items like cozy spaces and comfort foods, relationship resources like trusted family friends or relatives, and activity options that reliably improve mood and perspective.

Develop communication systems that work for your family's style and preferences, whether that involves regular check-ins, written notes, shared activities, or digital connections that maintain closeness despite busy schedules.

Build flexibility into your systems that allows for adaptation as your tween grows and circumstances change, because strategies that work perfectly at age eleven might need modification by age thirteen. Regular family evaluation of what's working and what needs adjustment prevents systems from becoming rigid and counterproductive.

Celebrate your family's unique strengths and characteristics rather than comparing your situation to other families who might appear to have easier circumstances. Every family faces challenges, and your particular combination of people creates both difficulties and advantages that are unique to you.

The Art of Good Enough Parenting

The myth of perfect parenting creates unnecessary stress and unrealistic expectations during an already challenging developmental phase. Good-enough parenting means meeting your child's essential needs while protecting your well-being and the household's ability to function —accepting that some aspects of daily life will be imperfect.

Recognize that your tween needs consistent love and support more than flawless execution of every parenting technique you've read about or heard from other families. Your genuine care and commitment matter more than the perfect implementation of expert advice that might not fit your specific situation.

Focus on essential priorities while letting less important issues slide when necessary, because energy and attention are finite resources that require strategic allocation. Maybe homework completion takes precedence over perfect room organization, or emotional support becomes more important than elaborate meal planning.

Allow yourself to make mistakes and model recovery rather than pretending that adults always know the right approach to novel situations. When you handle something poorly, acknowledge the error, make appropriate repairs, and demonstrate how people can learn from failures without being destroyed by them.

Adjust your expectations based on current family circumstances rather than maintaining standards that worked during easier periods or comparing your situation to that of families facing other challenges. Temporary modifications to rules, routines, or expectations might be necessary during particularly difficult phases.

Trust your instincts about your child and family while remaining open to new information and approaches that might improve your situation. You know your tween better than any expert, though outside perspectives can provide valuable insights that help you see familiar situations from a new angle.

Final Thoughts: You've Got This (Seriously)

You've now completed advanced training in tween survival, from understanding the biological forces that create daily chaos to developing strategies that help your family not just endure but actually thrive during this transformative period. Whether you feel like a confident expert or barely qualified amateur, you're exactly the parent your tween needs. Remember: this too shall pass, relationships can grow stronger through challenge, and teenagers eventually become grateful adults who might even admit you knew what you were doing.

The young person living in your home is fortunate to have someone committed to understanding their experience, supporting their development, and staying connected through their most challenging years. Your willingness to learn, adapt, and find humor in daily difficulties provides precisely what they need to navigate this transition successfully.

Remember that every family's journey through tweendom is different, and comparing your experience to others rarely offers a helpful perspective. Your particular combination of personalities, circumstances, and challenges creates a unique situation that requires customized approaches rather than universal solutions.

Trust the process, maintain your sense of humor, and know that countless families have successfully navigated these same challenges while building stronger relationships and raising children who become wonderful adults. You're part of a long tradition of parents who've discovered that surviving tweendom often involves more joy than expected.

Keep your expectations realistic, your snack drawer fully loaded, and your belief in your family's ability to grow stronger through these challenges. You're not just surviving daily chaos – you're raising a remarkable human being who will someday thank you for your patience, understanding, and willingness to love them through their most complicated years.

The tween years end, relationships recover from temporary strain, and families often discover that navigating this challenge together creates bonds that last a lifetime. You've got this, even when it doesn't feel that way, especially when it doesn't feel that way.

As I was finishing this book, Bash asked what it was about. I told him it was about parenting tweens. He thought about this and said, 'So it's about me being annoying?' I said it was about all the ways kids change during these years. He nodded. 'So yeah, I'm being annoying.' He paused. 'You should tell parents it gets better. Sometimes I'm not annoying.' High praise from a nine-year-old. I'll take it.

a small favor from one tired human to another

You just finished a whole book. That's basically a personal achievement.

If this book made you laugh, nod aggressively, feel seen, or whisper "OMG yes" into your coffee… would you do me a tiny favor?

If you've got **30 seconds**, leaving an Amazon review would mean a lot. Reviews help this book find other parents who need it — especially the ones currently debating whether "two-day-old hair" counts as a personality trait.

Two sentences is enough.

Seriously. No essay required.

Thank you for being here — and for helping this book reach more parents.

Scan QR Code here

eleven
bonus 1: f stands for...

A survival glossary for the tween years, organized by the only letter that truly captures this parenting phase.

You picked up a book called "What the Actual F?" so let's be honest about what that F really stands for. Spoiler: it stands for everything. Every frustration, every funny moment, every face-palm, every fleeting victory. Here's your alphabetical-within-the-alphabet guide to the F-words of tween parenting.

The Universal Fs

F is for "Feeding Frenzy" Growth spurts turn your refrigerator into a black hole. Bash can eat two grilled-cheese sandwiches after school and ask what's for dinner forty-five minutes later. Stock up or risk becoming the villain in a snack-supply horror story.

F is for "Fine" (The Word) The most suspicious word in the tween vocabulary. "Fine" can mean anything from genuine contentment to "my entire world is collapsing, but I'm not ready to talk about it." Learn to read the tone, the body language, and the door slam that follows.

F is for "Flat-Out Exhausted" After a day of tween negotiations, emotional ups and downs, and hygiene reminders, you'll feel like you ran a marathon in flip-flops. Naps aren't lazy – they're strategic recovery.

F is for "FOMO Fuel" Fear of missing out is real and expensive. Budget for the occasional "iconic moment," whether it's concert tickets or the right brand of water bottle that everyone apparently needs to survive sixth grade.

F is for "Forgive-and-Forget" Some days, they'll snap at you for crimes like existing in their vicinity or breathing too loudly. Breathe in, forgive fast, and remember that the sweet version of your kid is still in there somewhere.

F is for "Forget-O-Scope" Their memory for important things (permission slips, homework, dental appointments) vanishes faster than your patience. Their memory for that one embarrassing thing you said three years ago? Photographic.

F is for "Freedom Fail" Too much unsupervised time equals chaos. Start small – fifteen minutes alone without a snack raid or sibling incident counts as victory. Build from there.

F is for "Full-Blown Negotiator" They'll haggle over bedtime, screen time, and vegetable portions like they're brokering international treaties. Offer concessions wisely – one extra episode now might prevent a two-hour standoff later.

F is for "Feelings Firewall" Emotional walls go up faster than you can say, "What's wrong?" Deploy empathy and patience: "I get it – feelings can be overwhelming. Want to talk over pizza?" Pizza solves roughly 87% of tween crises.

F is for "Fake-It-'Til-You-Make-It" When they panic over a presentation or social situation, channel your inner confidence coach: "You got this. Eyes up, shoulders back." Even if you're sweating on their behalf.

Mara's Fs (The Girl Edition)

F is for "FaceTime" (Not the App) The real kind – eye-to-eye contact. When Mara says "Nothing's wrong" while avoiding my gaze, that's my cue for a gentle parental intervention. Sometimes I just sit near her and wait. Eventually, she talks.

F is for "Fashion Fiasco" Mara once insisted on wearing mismatched patterns that hurt my eyes. I let her express herself. The photos will be excellent blackmail material for her wedding slideshow.

F is for "Flare-Up" Puberty acne doesn't knock – it stages a hostile takeover, usually right before picture day. Treat those red invaders calmly, validate her frustration, and keep a gentle cleanser on standby.

F is for "Friendship Frenemy" One day they're BFFs posting heart emojis; the next day, someone's been "ghosted" for reasons that require a flowchart to understand. Keep your detective hat handy, but don't panic – drama passes faster than you can say "group chat."

F is for "Filter Fail" Mara's selfies involve twelve different filters, and half her face looks like a cartoon character. I've accepted that I will never understand the aesthetic, but I'm grateful she hasn't picked her senior photos yet.

F is for "Forty-Watt Wake-Up" Getting Mara out of bed looks like slow-motion footage of someone swimming through molasses. She has three alarms set. She sleeps through all of them. I've become the fourth alarm – the loud, annoying one that doesn't have a snooze button.

F is for "Forever Face-Mask" Mara's skincare routine could rival a chemistry lab. I let her mix, match, and marvel at the results, but I keep gentle backup products ready for when "natural remedies" go wrong.

F is for "Focus Fumble" With Mara's ADHD, focus comes and goes like WiFi in a storm. We've learned that what looks like "not trying" is usually her brain running twelve tabs at once. Patience and the proper support make all the difference.

F is for "Fashionably Late" Mara declares, "We have to leave in five minutes!" then, she vanishes into her room for twenty. I've learned to schedule everything thirty minutes earlier than necessary. It's the only way.

F is for "Future Therapist" She unloads her daily emotional saga on me, expecting that I'll nod sagely and say "That sounds really tough" approximately forty-seven times. I'm basically a counselor – working pro bono.

Bash's Fs (The Boy Edition)

F is for "Flatulence Follies" Bash thinks every room is his personal performance venue for bodily functions. We've invested in Febreze. Industrial quantities.

F is for "Fortnite Fiasco" "One more round" means three more hours. I've learned to set timers and accept that extracting him from a game requires the same skills as hostage negotiation.

F is for "Fridge Famine" We have a full fridge, a stocked pantry, and a nine-year-old who insists there's nothing to eat. Bash can consume a meal large enough to feed a small village, then wander into the kitchen an hour later asking what's for dinner. The answer is always the same: 'You just ate.' His response is always the same: 'But I'm hungry again.

F is for "Fidget Frenzy" Spinners, cubes, rubber bands, pen caps – if it can be clicked, twisted, or bounced, Bash has destroyed it. I find fidget toy casualties under the couch weekly.

F is for "Face-Plant Falls" Bash approaches physical activity with more enthusiasm than coordination. We've learned to keep frozen peas stocked at all times – they double as his favorite snack and our most-used ice pack. Sometimes he'll hold the bag over a fresh bruise while eating from it. Efficient, if nothing else.

F is for "Forgotten Homework" He swears he "did it the day before" or "turned it in already" with the confidence of someone who has never been caught in a lie. The Post-it note system helps. Slightly.

F is for "Foam Sword Duels" Every hallway is a battlefield, every stick is a weapon, and I am an acceptable target. I've learned to announce my presence before entering rooms.

F is for "Family-Group-Chat Phantom" Bash ghosts my texts faster than a Snapchat streak disappears. The only reliable way to get a response is to mention food.

F is for "Future-You Fear" He panics over things like they determine his entire life trajectory – a forgotten assignment, a friendship hiccup, a less-than-perfect grade. I tell him it'll all work out. He inherited my math skills, but unfortunately, he also inherited my tendency to overthink everything.

F is for "Fake Chore Offer" Bash is surprisingly helpful with chores – he just does them his own way. The dishes are done, but the silverware ends up in unusual places. The trash is taken out, but the new bag isn't put in. I've learned to appreciate the effort and quietly fix the details later.

And Finally...

F is for "F-You Ball" A DIY stress ball for when the chaos peaks. Squeeze it, breathe, remember that this phase is temporary. Bonus points if you label it honestly. No one will judge you. We've all been there.

F is for "Finally, They'll Thank You" Not today. Probably not tomorrow. But someday, years from now, they'll realize what you did for them during these chaotic years. They might even say it out loud. Until then, you've got this glossary – and the knowledge that every F-word moment is preparing both of you for what comes next.

twelve

bonus 2: tween slang decoder ring – when words mean everything except what you think

Reference Guide for the Linguistically Lost

Let's be honest: by the time you read this, at least half of these terms will be outdated. Mara has already informed me that some of the slang I learned last year is now considered "cheugy" (ironically, it is itself becoming obsolete). That's the nature of tween language – it evolves faster than you can Google it.

But here's the thing: you don't need to be fluent. You just need to understand enough to know when your kid is happy, sad, excited, or roasting you to your face with words you don't recognize. Think of this as a survival phrasebook, not a comprehensive dictionary.

A word of warning: do NOT attempt to use this slang yourself. When I tried to call dinner "bussin'," Bash stared at me like I'd committed a crime. Mara left the room. Sim pretended not to know me. Learn the words. Do not speak the words. You've been warned.

For a deeper dive into digital communication and why your tween speaks in hieroglyphics, see Chapter 5. This glossary is your quick-reference cheat sheet for decoding conversations in real time.

The Essentials: Words You'll Hear Daily

Slang	Meaning	Tween Usage	Parent Translation
Bet	Okay / Sure / Challenge accepted	"You can't finish that." "Bet."	They're agreeing or accepting a challenge.
Bussin'	Really good (especially food)	"This pizza is bussin'."	They like it. A lot.
Cap / No Cap	Lie / No lie	"That's cap." / "No cap, it's true."	They think you're lying, or they're emphasizing honesty.
Fire	Excellent, amazing	"That song is fire."	High praise. Accept the compliment.
GOAT	Greatest of All Time	"She's the GOAT."	Ultimate respect. Possibly about an athlete or a friend who shared snacks.
Lit	Amazing, fun, exciting	"That party was lit."	It was a good time. Don't ask for details.
Mid	Mediocre, underwhelming	"That movie was mid."	They're disappointed. It could also be applied to your cooking.
Slay	To succeed impressively	"You're gonna slay that test."	They're being supportive. Celebrate.
Sus	Suspicious, sketchy	"That's sus."	They don't trust it. It could be a person, a situation, or your excuse for being late.
Vibe	Atmosphere or feeling	"This place has good vibes."	They're assessing the mood. Trust their instincts.

EMOTIONAL EXPRESSIONS: Decoding How They Feel

Slang	Meaning	Tween Usage	Parent Translation
I'm dead / Dead	That's hilarious	"I'm dead 💀 "	They're laughing. Not actually deceased.
Big yikes	That's really embarrassing/bad	"Big yikes on that outfit."	Secondhand embarrassment. Possibly about you.
Hits different	Feels more meaningful than usual	"This song hits different at night."	They're having a moment. Don't interrupt.
It's giving...	It resembles or conveys	"It's giving desperate."	They're making a judgment. Brace yourself.
Mood	That's relatable	"Sleep is life. Mood."	They strongly identify with the statement.
Shook	Shocked, startled	"I'm shook."	Something surprised them. Ask gently.
Salty	Bitter, annoyed	"You're so salty about losing."	They're calling out resentment. Possibly yours.
Pressed	Upset, bothered	"Why are you so pressed?"	They think you're overreacting.
Living rent-free	Can't stop thinking about it	"That song is living rent-free in my head."	It's stuck. It could be good or bad.
Menty B	Mental breakdown	"Had a menty b over homework."	They were overwhelmed. Check in.

Social & Digital: Relationship Status Updates

Slang	Meaning	Tween Usage	Parent Translation
Ghosting	Cutting off communication suddenly	"He ghosted me."	Someone stopped responding. It hurts.
Left on read	Message seen but not replied to	"She left me on read."	They're feeling ignored. Validate this.
Stan	Obsessive fan	"I stan that singer."	Deep admiration. Expect merchandise requests.
Ship / Shipping	Supporting a romantic pairing	"I ship them so hard."	They want two people to date. It could be fictional or real.
Slide into DMs	Send a private message	"He slid into her DMs."	Someone made a move. Digitally.
Spill the tea	Share the gossip	"Spill the tea, what happened?"	They want information. Decide how much to share.
Throw shade	Subtle insult	"She threw shade at him."	Indirect criticism happened. Drama is brewing.
Clout	Influence or popularity	"She's doing it for clout."	They're questioning someone's motives.
Flex	Show off	"Nice flex."	Someone's bragging. Could be sincere or sarcastic.
Simp	Someone overly devoted	"He's simping for her."	They think someone is trying too hard romantically.

Reactions & Responses: Quick Translations

Slang	Meaning	Tween Usage	Parent Translation
Periodt	End of discussion	"I'm right, periodt."	They're not debating this. Let it go.
Facts	Absolutely true	"Facts."	Strong agreement.
Say less	I understand, no more explanation needed	"Say less, I got it."	They're on board. Stop talking.
W / L	Win / Loss	"That's a W."	They're rating outcomes. W is good, L is bad.
NGL	Not gonna lie	"NGL, that was awkward."	Honest admission incoming.
FR / FR FR	For real / For real for real	"FR, that's what happened."	They're emphasizing truth.
IYKYK	If you know, you know	"IYKYK 😌 "	Inside joke. You're probably not inside.
Lowkey / Highkey	Somewhat / Very much	"I lowkey want pizza."	Gauging intensity. Lowkey = a little. Highkey = a lot.
Ate that	Did something really well	"She ate that performance."	Strong compliment. Acknowledge their win.
Understood the assignment	Nailed it	"She understood the assignment."	Someone did exactly what they should have. Praise.

Final Note: When in Doubt, Just Ask

If your tween uses a word you don't recognize, it's okay to ask — just don't make it weird. A simple "What does that mean?" works better than pretending you understand or, worse, trying to use it yourself.

Mara has become my unofficial translator. She sighs heavily every time I ask, but I've noticed she also seems a little pleased to be the expert. Bash just laughs at me. Both responses are acceptable.

Remember: the specific words will keep changing, but the underlying goal stays the same — connection, expression, belonging. Focus on understanding what they're trying to communicate, not memorizing vocabulary that'll be obsolete by next semester.

And if all else fails, just nod and say "That's valid." It works in almost every situation. Trust me — I've tested it.

references

Marshall, W. A., & Tanner, J. M. (1969). "Variations in the Pattern of Pubertal Changes in Girls." Archives of Disease in Childhood, 44(235), 291–303.

Marshall, W. A., & Tanner, J. M. (1970). "Variations in the Pattern of Pubertal Changes in Boys." Archives of Disease in Childhood, 45(239), 13–23.

Mayo Clinic Staff. "Puberty: What's Happening to My Body?" MayoClinic.org.

Blakemore, S.-J., & Frith, U. (2005). The Learning Brain: Lessons for Education. Oxford University Press.

American Psychological Association. "Helping Your Teen Through Anxiety." APA.org

Faber, A., & Mazlish, E. (1980). How to Talk So Kids Will Listen & Listen So Kids Will Talk. Scribner.

Common Sense Media. "The Common Sense Census: Media Use by Tweens and Teens." CommonSenseMedia.org

Livingstone, S., & Smith, P. K. (2014). "Annual Research Review: Harms Experienced by Child Users of Online and Mobile Technologies." Journal of Child Psychology and Psychiatry, 55(6), 635–654.

Pew Research Center. "Teens, Social Media & Technology 2024." PewInternet.org

McCulloch, G. (2019). Because Internet: Understanding the New Rules of Language. Riverhead Books.

Danesi, M. (2017). The Semiotics of Emoji: The Rise of Visual Language in the Age of the Internet. Bloomsbury Academic.

Gottman, J. M., & Gottman, J. S. (2015). The Science of Trust: Emotional Attunement for Couples. W. W. Norton. (adaptable to parent–tween relationships)

Siegel, D. J., & Bryson, T. P. (2011). The Whole-Brain Child: 12 Revolutionary Strategies to Nurture Your Child's Developing Mind. Bantam.

Centers for Disease Control and Prevention. "Physical Activity Guidelines for Kids." CDC.gov

www.ingramcontent.com/pod-product-compliance
Lightning Source LLC
Chambersburg PA
CBHW071521120626
46550CB00006B/2312